Cara Cocking

Facility Location–Network Design Problems

Cara Cocking

Facility Location–Network Design Problems

Solution Approaches

Südwestdeutscher Verlag für Hochschulschriften

Impressum/Imprint (nur für Deutschland/ only for Germany)
Bibliografische Information der Deutschen Nationalbibliothek: Die Deutsche Nationalbibliothek verzeichnet diese Publikation in der Deutschen Nationalbibliografie; detaillierte bibliografische Daten sind im Internet über http://dnb.d-nb.de abrufbar.
Alle in diesem Buch genannten Marken und Produktnamen unterliegen warenzeichen-, marken- oder patentrechtlichem Schutz bzw. sind Warenzeichen oder eingetragene Warenzeichen der jeweiligen Inhaber. Die Wiedergabe von Marken, Produktnamen, Gebrauchsnamen, Handelsnamen, Warenbezeichnungen u.s.w. in diesem Werk berechtigt auch ohne besondere Kennzeichnung nicht zu der Annahme, dass solche Namen im Sinne der Warenzeichen- und Markenschutzgesetzgebung als frei zu betrachten wären und daher von jedermann benutzt werden dürften.

Verlag: Südwestdeutscher Verlag für Hochschulschriften Aktiengesellschaft & Co. KG
Dudweiler Landstr. 99, 66123 Saarbrücken, Deutschland
Telefon +49 681 37 20 271-1, Telefax +49 681 37 20 271-0, Email: info@svh-verlag.de
Zugl.: Heidelberg, Universitaet Heidelberg, 2008

Herstellung in Deutschland:
Schaltungsdienst Lange o.H.G., Zehrensdorfer Str. 11, D-12277 Berlin
Books on Demand GmbH, Gutenbergring 53, D-22848 Norderstedt
Reha GmbH, Dudweiler Landstr. 99, D- 66123 Saarbrücken
ISBN: 978-3-8381-0113-2

Imprint (only for USA, GB)
Bibliographic information published by the Deutsche Nationalbibliothek: The Deutsche Nationalbibliothek lists this publication in the Deutsche Nationalbibliografie; detailed bibliographic data are available in the Internet at http://dnb.d-nb.de.
Any brand names and product names mentioned in this book are subject to trademark, brand or patent protection and are trademarks or registered trademarks of their respective holders. The use of brand names, product names, common names, trade names, product descriptions etc. even without
a particular marking in this works is in no way to be construed to mean that such names may be regarded as unrestricted in respect of trademark and brand protection legislation and could thus be used by anyone.

Publisher:
Südwestdeutscher Verlag für Hochschulschriften Aktiengesellschaft & Co. KG
Dudweiler Landstr. 99, 66123 Saarbrücken, Germany
Phone +49 681 37 20 271-1, Fax +49 681 37 20 271-0, Email: info@svh-verlag.de

Copyright © 2008 Südwestdeutscher Verlag für Hochschulschriften Aktiengesellschaft & Co. KG and licensors
All rights reserved. Saarbrücken 2008

Produced in USA and UK by:
Lightning Source Inc., 1246 Heil Quaker Blvd., La Vergne, TN 37086, USA
Lightning Source UK Ltd., Chapter House, Pitfield, Kiln Farm, Milton Keynes, MK11 3LW, GB
BookSurge, 7290 B. Investment Drive, North Charleston, SC 29418, USA
ISBN: 978-3-8381-0113-2

Facility Location–Network Design Problems

Solution Approaches

Cara Cocking

To my sister Wendy

Abstract

This doctoral thesis presents new solution strategies for facility location–network design (FLND) problems. FLND is a combination of facility location and network design: the overall goal is to improve clients' access to facilities and the means of reaching this goal include both building facilities (as in facility location) and building travelable links (as in network design). We measure clients' access to facilities by the sum of the travel costs, and our objective is to minimize this sum. FLND problems have facility location problems and network design problems, both of which are $\mathcal{NP}$-hard, as subproblems and are therefore themselves theoretically difficult problems.

We approach the search for optimal solutions from both above and below, contributing techniques for finding good upper bounds as well as good lower bounds on an optimal solution.

On the upper bound side, we present the first heuristics in the literature for this problem. We have developed a variety of heuristics: simple greedy heuristics, a local search heuristic, metaheuristics including simulated annealing and variable neighborhood search, as well as a custom heuristic based on the problem-specific structure of FLND. Our computational results compare the performance of these heuristics and show that the basic variable neighborhood search performs the best, achieving a solution within 0.6% of optimality on average for our test cases.

On the lower bound side, we work with an existing IP formulation whose LP relaxation provides good lower bounds. We present a separation routine for a new class of inequalities that further improve the lower bound, in some cases even obtaining the optimal solution.

Putting all this together, we develop a branch-and-cut approach that uses heuristic solutions as upper bounds, and cutting planes for increasing the lower bound at each node of the problem tree, thus reducing the number of nodes needed to solve to optimality.

We also present an alternate IP formulation that uses fewer variables than the one accepted in the literature. This formulation allows some problems to be solved more quickly, although its LP relaxation is not as tight.

To aid in the visualization of FLND problem instances and their solutions, we have developed a piece of software, FLND Visualizer. Using this application one can create and modify problem instances, solve using a variety of heuristic methods, and view the solutions.

Finally, we consider a case study: improving access to health facilities in the Nouna health district of Burkina Faso. We demonstrate the solution techniques developed here on this real-world problem and show the remarkable improvements in accessibility that are possible.

Zusammenfassung

In der vorliegenden Arbeit leisten wir neue Lösungsmethoden für das Facility Location–Network Design (FLND) Problem. Dieses Problem ist eine Kombination aus Facility Location und Network Design: das Ziel ist es, den Zugang von Kunden zu gewissen Einrichtungen zu verbessern, sowohl durch das Bauen von Einrichtungen (wie im Facility Location Problem) als auch von Kanten (wie im Network Design Problem). Die Güte des Zugangs zu Einrichtungen entspricht der Summe der Reisekosten. Diese Summe gilt es zu minimieren. FLND Probleme enthalten Facility Location Probleme und Network Design Probleme, beide $\mathcal{NP}$-hard, als Subprobleme und sind daher selbst theoretisch schwere Probleme.

Wir leisten Beiträge zum Berechnen von guten oberen und unteren Schranken für optimale Lösungen.

Was obere Schranken betrifft, präsentieren wir die ersten Heuristiken überhaupt für dieses Problem. Wir haben verschiedene Heuristiken entwickelt: einfache Greedy Heuristiken, eine Local Search Heuristik, Metaheuristiken inklusive Simulated Annealing und Variable Neighborhood Search und auch eine Heuristik, die auf der problemspezifischen Struktur von FLND basiert. Rechenexperimente zeigen, dass die Basic Variable Neighborhood Search Heuristik die Beste ist, mit einer durchschnittlichen Lösungsqualität, die innerhalb von 0.6% von der optimalen Lösung liegt.

Was untere Schranken betrifft, gibt es schon eine IP Formulierung, deren LP Relaxierung gute Resultate liefert. Wir präsentieren aber Methoden für die Separierung von einer neue Klasse von Ungleichungen, die die unteren Schranken verbessern, manchmal sogar die optimale Lösung im Wurzelknoten finden.

Zudem erweitern wir eine branch-and-cut Methode, die Heuristiken für obere Schranken und Schnittebene für bessere untere Schranken an jedem Knoten des Problembaums verwendet. Die Anzahl der branch-and-cut Knoten wird dadurch stark reduziert.

Wir präsentieren auch eine neue IP Formulierung, die weniger Variablen hat. Diese Formulierung ermöglicht es, dass einige Probleme schneller gelöst werden können, obwohl die LP Relaxierung nicht so stark ist.

Um FLND Probleme und Lösungen visualisieren zu können, haben wir die Software FLND Visualizer entwickelt. Mit dieser Software kann man Probleme entwerfen und abändern, Heuristiken aufrufen, und Lösungen ansehen.

Schließlich machen wir eine Fallstudie: Das Ziel ist die Verbesserung des Zugangs zu Gesundheitseinrichtungen in Nouna, Burkina Faso. Wir verwenden die neuentwickelten Lösungsmethoden anhand dieses anwendungsnahen Problems und zeigen, dass bemerkenswerte Verbesserungen des Zugangs möglich sind.

Contents

Abbreviations	xi
Symbols and Notation	xi
List of Tables	xiii
List of Figures	xv
List of Algorithms	xvii

1 Introduction   1
  1.1 Problems and Methods 1
      1.1.1 Combinatorial Optimization 1
      1.1.2 Facility Location–Network Design 2
  1.2 Outline and Contributions 3
  1.3 Acknowledgments 4

2 Preliminaries and Terminology   7
  2.1 Sets and Graphs 7
  2.2 Complexity Theory 8
      2.2.1 Algorithms 8
      2.2.2 Problems 8
  2.3 Linear and Integer Programming 9
  2.4 Shortest Path Problems and Solutions 10
  2.5 Branch-and-Cut 11
      2.5.1 Branch-and-Bound 13
      2.5.2 The Cutting Plane Method 13
      2.5.3 Branch-and-Cut 14

3 Facility Location and Network Design   15
  3.1 Facility Location 15
      3.1.1 Median and Fixed Charge Problems 16
      3.1.2 Covering and Center Problems 17
  3.2 Network Design 19
      3.2.1 Inverse and Reverse Facility Location 20

	3.3	Facility Location–Network Design	21
		3.3.1 Disaggregate IP Formulation	24
		3.3.2 Aggregate IP Formulation	27
		3.3.3 Comparing IP Formulations	28

4 Upper Bound Approaches: Heuristics — 33
- 4.1 Greedy Heuristics — 35
- 4.2 A Custom Heuristic — 37
- 4.3 Neighborhoods and Neighbor Operators — 42
  - 4.3.1 Hamming Neighborhoods — 42
  - 4.3.2 Step Neighborhoods — 44
- 4.4 Local Search — 45
- 4.5 Simulated Annealing — 47
- 4.6 Variable Neighborhood Search Heuristics — 50
  - 4.6.1 Basic Variable Neighborhood Search — 51
  - 4.6.2 Reduced Variable Neighborhood Search — 53
  - 4.6.3 Variable Neighborhood Descent — 54
- 4.7 Comparison and Discussion — 56

5 Lower Bound Approaches — 65
- 5.1 Improving the LP Relaxation of D — 66
  - 5.1.1 Knapsack Cuts — 66
    - 5.1.1.1 Target Cut Method — 67
    - 5.1.1.2 Ones Plus Method — 68
  - 5.1.2 Results — 71
- 5.2 Improving the LP Relaxation of A — 73
  - 5.2.1 Subset Cuts — 74
  - 5.2.2 Similar Inequalities in the Literature — 76
  - 5.2.3 Results — 76
- 5.3 Comparison and Discussion — 77

6 Exact Approaches — 83
- 6.1 A Branch-and-Cut Solver — 83
- 6.2 Results — 84

7 A Case Study: Nouna — 87
- 7.1 The Setting: Nouna Health District — 87
- 7.2 Modeling as FLND — 90
- 7.3 Results — 92

8 Software: FLND Visualizer — 99
- 8.1 Creating Problem Instances — 99
- 8.2 Solving and Viewing Solutions — 101

9 Discussion and Conclusions — 105

A Test Instances	**107**
References	**119**

Abbreviations

FLND	Facility Location–Network Design	2
FL	Facility Location	15
IP	Integer Program (LP with integer variables)	2
LHS	Left-Hand Side of an inequality or equation	9
LP	Linear Program	9
ND	Network Design	19
RHS	Right-Hand Side of an inequality or equation	10
RVNS	Reduced Variable Neighborhood Search	53
VND	Variable Neighborhood Descent	54
VNS	Variable Neighborhood Search	50

Symbols and Notation

$|A|$	number of elements in a set	7
E	set of edges of a graph	7
$\mathcal{P}(A)$	the power set of set A, the set of all subsets of A	7
$\mathbb{R}$	real numbers	13
$\mathbb{R}^n$	vector space of dimension n with components from $\mathbb{R}$	13
V	set of nodes of a graph	7
$V \setminus U$	set difference: the elements of V that are not in U	7
x^*	fractional LP solution as point in a vector space	13

List of Tables

3.1	LP relaxation solution results	32
4.1	Comparison of all heuristics	59
4.2	Comparison of all heuristics' run times	59
4.3	Greedy, custom, local search, simulated annealing results	62
4.4	Variable neighborhood search results	63
5.1	Summary of LP relaxation gaps with no cuts added	65
5.2	Summary of lower bound gaps, D plus cuts	73
5.3	Summary of lower bound gaps, A plus cuts, budget FLND	78
5.4	Summary of lower bound gaps, A plus cuts, fixed charge FLND	79
5.5	Lower bound gaps, formulation D plus cuts	80
5.6	Lower bound gaps, formulation A plus cuts, budget FLND	81
5.7	Lower bound gaps, formulation A plus cuts, fixed charge FLND	82
6.1	Results summary, exact branch-and-cut solvers	85
6.2	Branch-and-cut results, number of nodes	86
7.1	Comparing FL, ND, and FLND on Nouna data	96
A.1	Problem instances	109
A.2	Problem instances	110

List of Figures

3.1	An FLND problem instance and solution	23
3.2	IP formulation variables	26
3.3	Comparing LP relaxation solutions for budget FLND	29
3.4	Comparing LP relaxation solutions for fixed charge FLND	30
3.5	Comparing solution times, aggregate vs. disaggregate IP	30
4.1	Greedy and custom heuristic results	40
4.2	Greedy and custom heuristic solution times	41
4.3	Local search and simulated annealing heuristic results	49
4.4	Local search and simulated annealing heuristic solution times	49
4.5	Simulated annealing, 0.99 versus 0.9999 temperature reduction	50
4.6	Basic variable neighborhood search heuristic results	53
4.7	Basic variable neighborhood search heuristic solution times	54
4.8	Reduced variable neighborhood search heuristic results	55
4.9	Reduced variable neighborhood search heuristic solution times	56
4.10	VND results shown with basic VNS	57
4.11	All VNS heuristic results shown together	58
4.12	Comparing all heuristics on one graph	60
4.13	Solution times of all heuristics on one graph	61
5.1	Depiction of a target cut	67
5.2	Lower bound gaps, D plus cuts	72
5.3	Lower bound gaps, A plus cuts, budget FLND	77
5.4	Lower bound gaps, A plus cuts, fixed charge FLND	78
5.5	Best lower bound gaps, A versus D, budget FLND	79
6.1	Number of nodes, branch-and-cut approaches	84
6.2	Branch-and-cut solve times	85
7.1	Burkina Faso	88
7.2	Nouna health district	89
7.3	Nouna FLND problem instance	91
7.4	Nouna solution starting with no facilities	93
7.5	Nouna solution, budget 200	94
7.6	Nouna solutions, plotting total travel cost versus budget	95
7.7	Nouna solution, budget 540	96

8.1	FLND Visualizer screen shot: creating	100
8.2	FLND Visualizer screen shot: creating	102
8.3	FLND Visualizer screen shot: solving	103
A.1	Problem instance 0A0a	111
A.2	Problem instance 0A2a	111
A.3	Problem instance 028a	112
A.4	Problem instance 220c	112
A.5	Problem instance 2A8c	113
A.6	Problem instance C20a	113
A.7	Problem instance S22b	114
A.8	Problem instance S22c	114
A.9	Problem instance 2A0b	115
A.10	Problem instance 2A0b, no potential edges shown	115
A.11	Problem instance CA2b	116
A.12	Problem instance CA2b, no potential edges shown	116
A.13	Problem instance SA8c	117
A.14	Problem instance SA8c, no potential edges shown	117

List of Algorithms

2.1	Dijkstra's single source shortest path algorithm.	12
4.1	Calculating total travel cost.	35
4.2	Greedy additive FLND heuristic.	36
4.3	Greedy subtractive FLND heuristic.	38
4.4	Custom FLND heuristic.	39
4.5	Random Hamming neighbor.	43
4.6	Best Hamming neighbor.	43
4.7	Random step neighbor.	45
4.8	Random initial solution.	46
4.9	Local search heuristic.	46
4.10	Simulated annealing heuristic.	48
4.11	Variable neighborhood search outline.	51
4.12	Basic variable neighborhood search heuristic.	52
4.13	Reduced variable neighborhood search heuristic.	55
4.14	Variable neighborhood descent heuristic.	57
5.1	Knapsack separation routine.	67
5.2	Target cuts method of making a knapsack cut.	68
5.3	Ones cut, knapsack cut with all 1 coefficients.	69
5.4	Ones plus method of making a knapsack cut.	70
5.5	Subset separation routine.	75

Chapter 1

Introduction

The impetus for this work came from the Nouna health district in Burkina Faso, Africa, population 275,000. In this district, there are no paved roads and people get around by foot, bicycle, or donkey. Medical facilities are limited, but there are 25 health centers scattered throughout the district that provide basic services. Some people prefer to see their village healer, whether out of superstition or convenience, rather than make the journey to a health center where they can be treated by trained medical personnel. During the rainy season, many roads become unusable and bicycle transport impossible. For those who decide to visit a health center in times of sickness, the route may be as long as 45 kilometers and involve walking in the mud and pouring rain for hours before the destination is reached. To be sure, the time and effort involved in simply getting to a health center is a deterrent for many in Nouna health district to seeking proper medical care.

The question that arises from this real scenario is, how can we make the health facilities more easily accessible to the people of Nouna health district? This doctoral thesis provides an answer to the question, in that it presents a variety of ways for solving the underlying mathematical problem. However, the thesis is more than that: the underlying problem is a general one with many and varied applications, besides being theoretically interesting as well, and the results presented here are not tied to any specific application context. The problem we are discussing is that of facility location–network design.

1.1 Problems and Methods

Facility location–network design problems will be discussed in detail in Chapter 3, but we explain the key concepts here briefly, along with typical solution approaches, in order to outline the context in which the contributions of this thesis are made.

1.1.1 Combinatorial Optimization

All the work contained herein falls under the more general label of combinatorial optimization. This field concerns itself with solving optimization problems over discrete structures, most often graphs. The solution techniques used come from both mathematics and computer science and in the grander scheme, combinatorial optimization as a discipline can be seen as lying at the fuzzy border between these two subjects.

For any given problem in combinatorial optimization, one of the first steps is usually to try to come up with an integer programming (IP) formulation. This provides a precise mathematical model of the problem, making it clear and well defined. The solving of the integer program by an IP solver, commercial or otherwise, can then provide a baseline for how difficult the problem is practically, what kinds of instances may be difficult, what sizes of instances can be solved, etc. For many problems, an IP solver cannot solve even moderately-sized instances in reasonable time or memory. Thus, more efficient solution techniques must be utilized.

One approach is to create heuristics, which may find a "good" solution to the problem, but often with no guarantee as to how close to optimal the produced solution is. In practice, many heuristics may get fairly close to optimal, as seen by comparing results on problem instances for which the optimal solution is known. If a guarantee is important, one can attempt to develop a heuristic for which something about the quality of the solutions produced can be proved, e.g., that any solution is no worse than a given constant factor of the optimal.

In terms of a minimization problem, heuristics provide an upper bound on any optimal solution. One can also approach the problem from the other side and try to find a lower bound on an optimal solution. This may be done by working with a relaxation of an IP formulation and adding cutting planes (inequalities that "cut" off nonoptimal, fractional solutions), or using other methods to get closer to the optimal solution.

Branch-and-bound is an exact solution technique that proceeds by creating a tree of nodes. The original problem is at the root node and subproblems are created such that if all the subproblems are solved, the original problem will be solved. Branch-and-cut is a method that combines branch-and-bound and cutting planes, using cutting planes at each node in the tree to try to reach an optimal solution with fewer subproblems. All of these methods will be discussed in more detail in the next two chapters.

1.1.2 Facility Location–Network Design

As is suggested by the name, facility location–network design (FLND) combines facility location and network design. Facility location deals with optimally locating facilities. There are two main parties involved in any facility location problem: the facilities themselves and the clients of the facilities. Typically we want the facilities to be close to the clients, which can be defined in several ways. We may or may not have other constraints, such as a limitation on the number of facilities to build or maximum capacities on each facility.

Because we deal only with discrete facility location here, the problems are represented using graphs. The nodes of the graph are the union of the clients and the possible facility locations, and edges represent the ability to travel from one node to another and are the means by which clients reach facilities. A node may represent both a client and a potential facility location.

In network design, the basic problem is to optimally construct a network that enables some kind of flow, and possibly that satisfies some additional constraints. The nodes are given and the network is constructed from a set of potential edges, or links. In our case, the flow involved is that between clients and facilities.

The objective in any of these problems, or how we measure optimality, can vary. A common objective in facility location is to minimize the total travel costs, and this is the objective that we primarily consider in this thesis. In facility location–network design, the objective may be met using the means of both facility location and network design, i. e., by building both facilities and links.

1.2 Outline and Contributions

The remainder of this thesis is structured as follows: In Chapter 2 we review some facts and methods from graph theory, complexity theory, linear and integer programming, as well as the branch-and-cut approach. These concepts will be helpful in understanding the rest of the thesis.

In Chapter 3 we introduce and precisely define the facility location–network design problems that we consider, including more detailed presentations of the two underlying subfields of facility location and network design. We describe an IP formulation for FLND that can be found in the literature, and present an alternate formulation of our own that uses fewer variables.

Chapter 4 contains all of the heuristic methods we have designed, which produce upper bounds on the solutions of FLND problems. To our knowledge, there are no heuristics in the literature specifically for FLND problems; these are all new contributions. The heuristics we have developed include simple greedy heuristics, a local search heuristic, adaptation of the metaheuristics simulated annealing and variable neighborhood search, as well as a custom heuristic based on the problem-specific structure of FLND. For the heuristics that operate based on neighborhoods, we have developed two different neighbor operators, which we also present. We give computational results comparing the performance of the heuristics to each other as well as to known optimal solution values.

To address the lower bounds, in Chapter 5 the focus is on improving the LP (linear programming) relaxations of the two IP formulations given in Chapter 3. We consider each formulation separately and develop additional valid inequalities and related separation routines that improve the lower bounds as compared with solving the LP relaxation without strengthening. Computational results showing the effectiveness of the cuts are given, and the final lower bounds obtained from both formulations are compared.

Chapter 6 considers exact approaches to solving FLND problems. We develop a comprehensive branch-and-cut solver that uses heuristics from Chapter 4 to get good upper bounds and separation routines from Chapter 5 that produce cutting planes, allowing us to raise the local lower bound at each node of the problem tree. Computational results show how the number of nodes reduces when using our branch-and-cut solver, as compared with the generic branch-and-cut that takes place when solving the integer program with a commercial solver.

A special treat awaits in Chapter 7 where we examine a case study. One of the initial stimuli for this line of research was the desire to improve access to health facilities in the Nouna health district of Burkina Faso. Here we demonstrate our solution techniques on this real-world problem and show the remarkable improvements in accessibility that are possible.

Finally in Chapter 8 we present a sophisticated software application, FLND Visualizer, that can be used to work visually with FLND problems. It allows the creation, modification, and saving of problem instances; solving using various heuristics; and viewing and saving of solutions.

The last chapter, Chapter 9, comprises a summary, conclusions, and discussion of future research directions.

Appendix A details the characteristics of the test instances used throughout this thesis.

Here we summarize the contributions of this doctoral thesis:

- A new IP formulation for FLND that uses fewer variables than the existing formulation in the literature, plus a class of valid inequalities that greatly strengthens its initially weak LP relaxation.

- An assortment of heuristics for FLND problems (the first in the literature), including greedy, local search, simulated annealing, variable neighborhood search, and custom heuristics.

- A valid class of inequalities and separation routine, to be used with the standard LP relaxation, that produces better lower bounds for FLND problems than any other methods in the literature.

- A branch-and-cut solver for FLND (the first in the literature), incorporating the new upper and lower bound methods developed, that can solve problems using fewer nodes than commercial IP solvers.

- A sophisticated software application for working visually with FLND problems.

1.3 Acknowledgments

Many people have contributed to this work directly and indirectly through technical discussions and guidance as well as nontechnical support and encouragement.

The first thanks go to my advisor, Gerhard Reinelt, for providing me with a spot in his work group and for all the support and direction along the way on my doctoral journey.

1.3. ACKNOWLEDGMENTS

The members of my work group provided a pleasant working atmosphere: Dino Ahr, Thorsten Bonato, Marcus Oswald, Hanna Seitz, Chotiros Surapholchai, Dirk Theis, Khoa Vo, and Klaus Wenger. Special thanks to Marcus Oswald for fruitful technical discussions related to the cuts presented in Chapter 5.

Our secretaries, Catherine Proux and Karin Tenschert, and our system administrator, Georgios Nikolis, took care of administrative needs and kept the machines running, and also contributed to the positive working environment.

I thank Buchheim, Liers, and Oswald for providing their target cuts code for my use (Chapter 5).

For the chance to apply this work to improving the accessibility of health facilities in Nouna health district (discussed in Chapter 7), I owe gratitude to many people. Steffen Flessa proposed the idea and provided support and guidance throughout. While working on the Nouna project, various colleagues in Heidelberg provided advice and support: Manuela De Allegri, Mamadou Mariko, Tin Tin Su, Martina Weiss, and Yazoumé Yé.

At the CRSN (Nouna Health Research Center) in Nouna itself, a number of people helped me in my efforts to collect data and learn about the situation first hand during my visit: Kadi Djim, Bocar Kouyaté, Dimitri Poda, Mamadou Sanon, Seraphin Simboro, and Maurice Yé. Special thanks to Mamadou Sanon for serving as my daily guide and translator for the two weeks I was in Nouna.

Thanks to various friends and family for providing encouragement: Richard and Doris Cocking, Wendy Adkins, Peter DePasquale, Catherine Foss, Daphne Pediaditakis, and Douglas Tang.

Finally, thanks to all who proofread parts of my dissertation: Thorsten Bonato, Marcus Oswald, Hanna Seitz, Douglas Tang, Khoa Vo, and Klaus Wenger.

Chapter 2

Preliminaries and Terminology

In this chapter we review some concepts from graph theory, complexity theory, and linear and integer programming, as well as the branch-and-cut approach. These concepts constitute a body of knowledge that helps in understanding the rest of the thesis and are used throughout. Concepts with a more limited scope will be defined later, as needed.

2.1 Sets and Graphs

A **set** is a collection of distinct elements. The standard operations set union, set intersection, and set difference ($\{a,b\} \setminus \{a,c\} = \{b\}$) apply.

If set A is a subset of set B, we write $A \subseteq B$. The **empty set**, denoted $\emptyset$, is a subset of every set. The **power set** of a set, denoted $\mathcal{P}(A)$, is the set of all subsets. The number of elements in a set A is indicated by $|A|$, and we have $|\mathcal{P}(A)| = 2^{|A|}$.

An **undirected graph** $G = (V, E)$ consists of a nonempty set V of **nodes** and a set E of **edges**. The nodes of G may be denoted $V(G)$ and the edges of G may be denoted $E(G)$. An edge of an undirected graph is an unordered pair of distinct nodes, each of which is called an **endnode**. We denote an edge with endnodes u and v by uv, and have $uv = vu$. If there is an edge between two nodes u and v, those nodes are said to be **adjacent** and are called **neighbors**. Note that we disallow **parallel edges**, i.e., there can be at most one edge with endnodes u and v. When discussing graphs in the scope of this thesis, we are always referring to undirected graphs (no parallel edges, no loops), unless otherwise stated.

A **path** in a graph is a set of edges $\{v_0v_1, v_1v_2, ...v_{n-1}v_n\}$ where all of the nodes, v_i, along the path are pairwise distinct. In a graph with edge weights d_{uv} associated with every edge $uv \in E$, the **length** of a path is the sum of the edge weights on the edges of the path,

$$\sum_{i=0}^{n-1} d_{v_i v_{i+1}}.$$

7

A graph is said to be **connected** if for every pair of nodes u and v, there is a path from u to v. A **complete graph** is one such that every pair of nodes is an edge of the graph.

2.2 Complexity Theory

In this section we introduce concepts that enable us to discuss the relative efficiency of algorithms as well as to get an idea of how difficult a problem might be in practice.

2.2.1 Algorithms

Though space complexity may also come into play, we are primarily interested in time complexity. The **time complexity** of an algorithm is a function on the size of the input to an algorithm giving the time requirements of the algorithm. The time requirements are expressed by the number of basic steps to be performed, such as on a modern computer. Time complexity is not concerned with how long an algorithm takes to run, but rather it captures the notion of how the running time *grows* as the size of the input grows. For example, if the function n^2 describes the time complexity of a particular algorithm, then doubling the size of the input increases the run time by a factor of 4.

We generally use big-oh notation to describe time complexity and this is a worst-case measure. A function $f(n)$ is $O(g(n))$ whenever there exists a constant c such that $f(n) \leq c*g(n)$ for all values of $n \geq 0$. Given this definition, an algorithm that is $O(n^2)$ is also $O(n^3)$, but we use the smallest time complexity function $g(n)$ that we can in describing time complexity.

A **polynomial time algorithm** is one whose time complexity function can be bounded by a polynomial, e.g., $O(n)$, $O(nlogn)$, or $O(n^5)$. Algorithms of this sort are generally considered efficient. Any algorithm whose time complexity cannot be bounded by a polynomial, e.g., $O(2^n)$, $O(3^n)$, or $O(n!)$, is said to be an **exponential time algorithm** and is considered inefficient. For small values of n, the difference in actual running time between a polynomial time algorithm and an exponential time algorithm may be negligible; but as n increases, the difference becomes huge, as in a few minutes versus centuries, or even billions of years.

2.2.2 Problems

In complexity theory, classes of problems are based on decision problems. A **decision problem** is one that has a yes or no answer. In this work we are interested in optimization problems, but any optimization problem has an associated decision problem. In general, for a cost minimization problem, we have the associated decision problem, "Does there exist a solution with cost no more than B?"

The complexity class $\mathcal{P}$ contains those decision problems that can be solved in polynomial time. For a problem Π, if there exists a polynomial time algorithm that solves Π, then $\Pi \in \mathcal{P}$. Problems in $\mathcal{P}$ are the "easier" problems.

The complexity class $\mathcal{NP}$ requires more explanation. A decision problem is said to be in $\mathcal{NP}$ if a yes instance can be verified in polynomial time. For example, consider the decision problem version of the famous traveling salesman problem: given a set of cities, distances between all the cities, and a bound B, is there a tour of length not more than B? To prove that the answer is yes for a given problem instance, one could produce a tour with length not more than B. Then to verify that this is a yes instance, we need only examine the given tour and confirm that its length is not more than B, which can easily be done in polynomial time.

Clearly, $\mathcal{P} \subseteq \mathcal{NP}$. It is not known, but is strongly suspected, that $\mathcal{P} \neq \mathcal{NP}$. If this is the case, then some problems in $\mathcal{NP}$ are not in $\mathcal{P}$, and these problems are the "harder" problems. Stephen Cook, one of the pioneers of complexity theory, proved in 1971 that the satisfiability problem is the "hardest" problem in $\mathcal{NP}$ [C71]. More precisely, his result means that if the satisfiability problem can be solved in polynomial time, so can every other problem in $\mathcal{NP}$, and likewise, if some other problem in $\mathcal{NP}$ cannot be solved in polynomial time, then neither can the satisfiability problem. In the meantime, other problems have been shown to share this property with the satisfiability problem, and these "hardest" problems in $\mathcal{NP}$ belong to the class of $\mathcal{NP}$-**complete** problems.

The term $\mathcal{NP}$-**hard** is used to refer to the class of optimization problems whose corresponding decision problem is $\mathcal{NP}$-complete. These are problems for which there is no known polynomial time algorithm and attempts at finding one would likely be misplaced. These are difficult problems. The FLND problems studied in this thesis are all $\mathcal{NP}$-hard.

2.3 Linear and Integer Programming

Linear programming (LP) and **integer programming** (IP) are ways of formulating optimization problems. A linear program can be written in the following form:

$$\text{Minimize} \quad \sum_j c_j x_j \qquad (2.1)$$

$$\text{Subject to} \quad \sum_j a_{ij} x_j \geq b_i \quad \forall i \qquad (2.2)$$

$$x_j \geq 0 \quad \forall j \qquad (2.3)$$

The a_{ij}, b_i, and c_j are constants and the x_j are variables over the real numbers. The first line (2.1) is the **objective function** and specifies the linear function to be minimized. The minimization (or more generally, optimization) takes place subject to a set of **constraints**, expressed in the succeeding lines (2.2) and (2.3). When discussing a constraint, or any inequality, we can refer to its parts as the **left-hand side (LHS)**, which contains all the variables involved, and the **right-hand side (RHS)**, which is a constant.

In other notation, the constraints may be expressed $Ax \leq b$ where A is a matrix and x and b are vectors, all with appropriate dimensions. Any vector x satisfying this system of inequalities is a **feasible solution**. The goal is to find an **optimal solution** according to the objective.

In a **linear program**, as well as in an integer program (sometimes called an integer linear program), the objective function and all the constraints must be linear. The variables in a linear program take on real-number values, possibly with upper and lower bounds. If some or all of the variables should be restricted to integer values, then we have an **integer program**, also known as a mixed integer program.

While the problem of integer programming is $\mathcal{NP}$-hard and generally difficult to solve, linear programming is solvable in polynomial time. Linear programs can be solved efficiently in practice as well, using methods such as the simplex algorithm [D51], which, ironically, despite its excellent performance in practice, has exponential worst-case time complexity.

If we drop some constraints from a problem, we are **relaxing** it. Given an integer program, if we relax the integrality constraints, we get an LP which is called the **LP relaxation** of the IP. In a minimization problem, solving the LP relaxation gives us a lower bound on the optimal solution value of the IP.

Commercial as well as free solvers for mathematical programming problems, including LPs and IPs, exist. In this work, we employ the use of the commercial solver CPLEX version 8.1, by ILOG [CPLEX].

2.4 Shortest Path Problems and Solutions

A subproblem that comes up frequently in this work is the shortest path problem. Given a graph $G = (V, E)$ with positive edge weights d_{ij} for each $ij \in E$ and two nodes s and t, the **shortest path problem** is to find the shortest path in G from s to t. The **single source shortest path problem** takes a single node $s \in V$ as input and the goal is to find the shortest path from every node in G to s, or equivalently, from s to every node in G. In an **all pairs shortest path problem**, the shortest paths between all pairs of nodes in G are to be found. Shortest path problems belong to the complexity class $\mathcal{P}$ and thus can be solved in polynomial time.

The shortest path problem can be formulated as an LP. Here, d_{ij} are the edge weights and the variables x_{ij} take on the value 1 if edge ij is in the shortest path and 0 otherwise. They can also be thought of as flow variables. Given that node s is the initial node and t is the node to which we want to find the shortest path, we can imagine one unit of flow leaving s and needing to find the shortest way to t. As such, the shortest path problem may be structured as a minimum cost network flow problem. The LP formulation follows:

2.5. BRANCH-AND-CUT

$$\text{Minimize} \quad \sum_i \sum_j d_{ij} x_{ij} \quad (2.4)$$

$$\text{Subject to} \quad \sum_j x_{ji} - \sum_k x_{ik} = \begin{cases} -1 & i = s \\ 1 & i = t \\ 0 & \text{otherwise} \end{cases} \quad \forall i \quad (2.5)$$

$$x_{ij} \geq 0 \quad \forall i, j \quad (2.6)$$

The objective (2.4) is to minimize the length of the path. Constraints (2.5) are the "flow" constraints. For each node i, the difference between flow in and flow out should be 0, unless $i = s$ in which case there is one unit of outgoing flow, or $i = t$ in which case there is one unit of incoming flow. The x_{ij} variables were conceived of as binary variables, but because the constraint matrix is totally unimodular, we are guaranteed to have integer solutions even if we solve this as an LP instead of an IP, thus in (2.6) we require only that the x_{ij} be greater than or equal to zero instead of integral.

Although not the most efficient way to solve the shortest path problem, this LP is the basis for the integer programming formulations of FLND that we will present in the next chapter.

Shortest path problems can be solved more efficiently with specialized algorithms such as Dijkstra's algorithm. Shown in Algorithm 2.1, DIJKSTRA solves the single source shortest path problem from source node s on a graph G with the weight of each edge $ij \in E(G)$ given by the weight function $d(i, j)$. As a notational aside, we may leave off d as a parameter in calling DIJKSTRA when the weights are simply fixed travel costs d_{ij} on each edge, and considered part of the graph.

The algorithm begins with the node s and branches out, ultimately forming a **shortest path tree** rooted at s, i.e., a tree in which the unique path from any node to s is the shortest path in G. The set S contains nodes already scanned and Q contains nodes still to be scanned. Traditionally, Q is initialized with all the nodes in the graph, but we add nodes only as we encounter them. This allows us to easily detect cases where G is not connected, and we return this information as a boolean value. If G is not connected, not every node will have a shortest path to s.

After the algorithm completes, the arrays *track* and *len* contain the shortest path tree information. For a given node v, *track*[v] contains the next node in the path from v to s and *len*[v] contains the length of the path from v to s.

Many of the FLND heuristics that we present in Chapter 4 use Dijkstra's algorithm as a subroutine.

2.5 Branch-and-Cut

Branch-and-cut is a method for solving combinatorial optimization problems that combines branch-and-bound and cutting planes. In our discussion of these methods, we assume a minimization problem.

Algorithm 2.1 Dijkstra's single source shortest path algorithm.

DIJKSTRA(G, d, s)
1   INITIALIZE-DIJKSTRA(G, s)
2   $S \leftarrow \emptyset$
3   $Q \leftarrow \{s\}$
4   **while** $Q \neq \emptyset$
5   **do** $u \leftarrow$ node in Q with smallest $len[u]$
6           $Q \leftarrow Q \setminus \{u\}$
7           $S \leftarrow S \cup \{u\}$
8   **for** each node $nei \notin S$ adjacent to u
9   **do if** $len[nei] > len[u] + d(u, nei)$
10   **then** $len[nei] \leftarrow len[u] + d(u, nei)$
11                      $track[nei] \leftarrow u$
12                      $Q \leftarrow Q \cup \{nei\}$
13 **return** $|S| == |V(G)|$

INITIALIZE-DIJKSTRA(G, s)
1   **for** each node $v \in V(G)$
2   **do** $track[v] \leftarrow v$
3           $len[v] \leftarrow \infty$
4   $len[s] \leftarrow 0$

2.5.1 Branch-and-Bound

Branch-and-bound is an exact solution technique that proceeds by creating a tree of nodes, called the **branch-and-bound tree**. The original problem is at the root node and subproblems are created such that if all the subproblems are solved, the original problem will be solved. During **branching**, subproblems are typically formed by fixing variables. For example, if a binary variable x is the selected **branching variable**, then two subproblems are created: one in which x is fixed to the value 0, and one in which x is fixed to the value 1.

During the process, the best feasible solution found thus far is maintained, and this provides a **global upper bound** on the problem. At each node, an attempt is made to solve the subproblem, and if successful, may give a new global upper bound. In case of success there is no need to continue branching on that node and we say the subproblem is **fathomed**.

Another way to fathom a node is via lower bounds. At each node, lower bounds on the subproblem are calculated by solving the LP relaxation, and these are **local lower bounds** because they are only valid for the given node. If at some node, the local lower bound is higher than the global upper bound, then we know that this branch of the tree will not produce an optimal solution; the node is fathomed and we do not need to pursue it any farther.

Finally, if we determine that there is no feasible solution at a given node, then the node can be fathomed. If it is not possible to fathom a node, then we branch and create subproblems.

When all open subproblems have been fathomed, the best feasible solution found is optimal.

2.5.2 The Cutting Plane Method

To more precisely describe the cutting plane method, we first introduce some polyhedral theory.

We denote the set of real numbers $\mathbb{R}$, and $\mathbb{R}^n$ a vector space of dimension n with components from $\mathbb{R}$. The set of feasible solutions to a linear program $\{x \in \mathbb{R}^n \mid Ax \leq b\}$ forms a **polyhedron**. An inequality is **valid** with respect to polyhedron P if every point in P satisfies the inequality. In general, for a point $x \notin P$, a **cutting plane** is an inequality that separates x from P. That is, the cutting plane, or **cut** for short, is valid for P but **violated** by x.

Recall that a relaxation of a problem relaxes (or removes) some constraints, thus creating a bigger solution space. The **cutting plane method** works as follows: Suppose P is the polyhedron representing the convex hull of the feasible solution points of a given combinatorial optimization problem Π that has been formulated as an integer program. Relaxing the integer constraints produces the polyhedron Q. Now suppose $x^* \in Q$ is the solution to the LP relaxation. If $x^* \notin P$ then there exists a cut that **separates** x^* from P. A **separation procedure** searches for such a cut. When found, this cut is added to the LP and it is solved again, producing a new x^* whose objective function value (local lower bound if a branch-and-cut subproblem is being solved) has hopefully increased, and the process is repeated.

The separation procedure is a very important piece of the cutting plane method and finding good cuts (or any cuts at all) can be difficult and time-consuming. A separation procedure that searches within a particular class of valid inequalities is a separation procedure for that class. If the procedure always finds a violated inequality if one exists, then it is called **exact**, otherwise it is called **heuristic**.

In Chapter 5 we discuss separation procedures used to improve the lower bound on FLND problems.

2.5.3 Branch-and-Cut

Branch-and-cut is based on branch-and-bound, with the addition of the cutting plane method at each node of the problem tree to increase the local lower bound of the node, perhaps leading to the subproblem being fathomed. With the branch-and-cut approach, fewer nodes need be explored than with branch-and-bound.

The commercial solver CPLEX uses branch-and-cut to solve IPs. The process begins with a branch-and-bound tree, and includes various classes of cuts, which may be turned on or off by the user, that are introduced at the nodes if CPLEX thinks they might be helpful. CPLEX also provides facilities for programmers to write their own problem-specific separation routines for generating cuts, and we make use of these facilities in this work, as described in Chapter 5.

For further details on the topics covered in this chapter, see the references below.

Graph theory	Diestel [D06]
Complexity theory	Garey and Johnson [GJ79]
Linear programming	Chvátal [C83]
Integer programming	Wolsey [W98]
Algorithms	Cormen, et al. [CLRS01]
Branch-and-cut	Jünger, Reinelt, and Thienel [JRT95]

Chapter 3

Facility Location and Network Design

We now describe facility location and network design individually, and then we define facility location–network design (FLND) and give two IP formulations for FLND.

3.1 Facility Location

"Location, location, location." This popular phrase in real estate emphasizes the most important factor in the market value of a home. Everyone can appreciate the importance of location, whether it's the location of a home, office, store, warehouse, or garbage dump. Location decisions arise frequently in both private and public sectors, and the results of these decisions can have a large impact on whether the enterprise succeeds or fails. As an aid to decision making, the field of facility location provides tools and methods for finding locations that are optimal in the mathematical sense with respect to quantifiable factors.

Modern discrete facility location began as a field in the 1960s [H64, H65, M64, TB68]. The goal in a facility location problem is to find the optimal locations for **facilities**, but little more can be said that is common to all facility location problems. In the course of time, many variations in the problems have developed and the details vary widely. We will discuss only those varieties that are most relevant to the work presented here. For a more general overview of discrete facility location, see Daskin [D95].

In addition to the facilities, the **clients** of the facilities make up an important part of any problem. Usually we want the facilities to be close to the clients and we use some quantification of "closeness" to weigh feasible solutions against one another. For example, we might be interested in locating a hospital in a region. The hospital is the facility and the people living in the towns in the region are the (prospective) clients of the hospital. We could judge a potential hospital location by the sum of the distances from the hospital to each town in the region. Clearly an optimal location is one with minimum sum.

When we represent these problems as a graph, the nodes make up the clients as well as the potential facility locations, and the edges represent a connection between two nodes and are often weighted with travel or delivery costs. The nodes may be weighted with the **demand** that each represents, such as the population of a town.

In the ensuing subsections we discuss some facility location problems as characterized by their objectives.

3.1.1 Median and Fixed Charge Problems

Some of the earliest problems studied in facility location were **median problems**, also known as minisum problems, in which the objective is the minimization of the sum of the travel costs [H64, H65, M64]. In the classic p-median problem, the number of facilities to locate, p, is given. The problem may be defined mathematically as follows: We are given a set of clients I and a set of potential facility sites J, the demands at each client a_i, and distances d_{ij} between every client and facility. The sets I and J may be disjoint, overlapping, or the same. The problem is to locate p facilities such that the total demand-weighted travel cost is minimized. That is, find a set $K \subseteq J$, $|K| = p$, that minimizes the sum $\sum_{i \in I} a_i \min_{j \in K} d_{ij}$.

Two notable points here are that (1) the distances between every pair of nodes must be determined beforehand, and (2) each client is assigned to its nearest facility. If a noncomplete graph is given, the distances can be calculated by finding the shortest path between every pair of nodes. Assigning each client to its nearest facility is clearly necessary in an optimal solution, and this is always possible because we are dealing with **uncapacitated** facilities, i.e., there is no limit on how much demand a facility can handle.

A standard IP formulation for the p-median problem is given below.

$$\text{Minimize} \quad \sum_{i \in I} \sum_{j \in J} a_i d_{ij} x_{ij}$$

$$\text{Subject to} \quad \sum_{j \in J} x_{ij} = 1 \qquad \forall i \in I \qquad (3.1)$$

$$x_{ij} \leq z_j \qquad \forall i \in I \; \forall j \in J \qquad (3.2)$$

$$\sum_{j \in J} z_j = p \qquad (3.3)$$

$$x_{ij}, z_j \in \{0, 1\} \qquad \forall i \in I \; \forall j \in J$$

The binary variables z_j represent whether or not a facility is located at j and x_{ij} whether client i is assigned to facility j. Constraints (3.1) assign each client to exactly one facility, (3.2) ensure that a client is assigned only to an open facility, and (3.3) opens exactly p facilities.

3.1. FACILITY LOCATION

The structure of the p-median problem implicitly assumes that the cost of building a facility is the same at all sites. **Fixed charge problems** have the same goal, i.e., minimizing the total travel cost, but potential facilities j have fixed charges f_j associated with them, and these costs can vary by location. The fixed facility construction costs are added into the objective so that the goal is to minimize total costs. The number of facilities built is determined endogenously by the problem.

A classic problem of this type is the uncapacitated facility location problem, also known as the simple plant location problem. The objective is to minimize the sum of the fixed costs and (demand-weighted) travel costs. To formulate this problem we start with the p-median formulation, remove the constraint (3.3) limiting the number of facilities to p, and replace the objective with

$$\text{Minimize} \sum_{j \in J} f_j z_j + \sum_{i \in I} \sum_{j \in J} a_i d_{ij} x_{ij}$$

3.1.2 Covering and Center Problems

An alternative to median problems that is used frequently in public facility location is **covering problems**. In these problems, we introduce the notion of **coverage** and say that a client is **covered** if it has a facility located within a given distance or travel cost. We mention these problems because they are an important alternative to median problems, but they are not the focus of this thesis.

In the **set covering problem**, the entire demand must be covered and the goal is to minimize the number of facilities used in doing so. To formulate the problem, we let N_i refer to the set of facility sites that would cover client i, so if D is the coverage distance we are given, then $N_i = \{j \mid d_{ij} \leq D\}$. Then using the same notation as in the previous subsection, the IP can be written as follows:

$$\text{Minimize} \quad \sum_{j \in J} z_j \tag{3.4}$$

$$\text{Subject to} \quad \sum_{j \in N_i} z_j \geq 1 \quad \forall i \in I \tag{3.5}$$

$$z_j \in \{0,1\} \quad \forall j \in J$$

The objective (3.4) is to minimize the number of facilities placed and constraints (3.5) ensure that every client is covered.

The **maximum covering problem** includes a limit on the number of facilities to locate and attempts to maximize demand coverage using the given number of facilities. It can be formulated as follows:

$$\text{Maximize} \quad \sum_{i \in I} a_i y_i \tag{3.6}$$

$$\text{Subject to} \quad y_i \leq \sum_{j \in N_i} z_j \quad \forall i \in I \tag{3.7}$$

$$\sum_{j \in J} z_j = p \tag{3.8}$$

$$y_i, z_j \in \{0,1\} \quad \forall i \in I \; \forall j \in J$$

We have introduced a new variable: y_i takes on the value 1 if client i is covered and 0 otherwise. The objective (3.6) is to maximize demand-weighted coverage, and constraints (3.7) set the y_i variables appropriately so that a client i is marked as covered only if one of the facilities in its set N_i is opened.

The p-center problem is closely related to the set covering problem as well as to the p-median problem. In a **center problem**, also known as a minimax problem, the goal is to minimize the maximum distance between a client and its nearest facility. The inputs to a p-center problem are the same as to a p-median problem, except that the demands of each client are irrelevant. To create an IP formulation, we replace the objective of the p-median formulation with

$$\text{Minimize } y$$

and add an additional set of constraints:

$$\sum_{j \in J} d_{ij} x_{ij} \leq y \quad \forall i \in I$$

The relation between p-center and set covering should be clear: In the former we fix the number of facilities and determine the maximum distance between a client and its nearest facility. In the latter we fix the maximum distance between a client and its nearest facility and determine the number of facilities needed.

Any of the facility location problems discussed in this section could also have capacities involved, which makes the problem a bit different. In **capacitated** problems, we allow capacity restrictions on the facilities and have additional inputs C_j, the maximum demand that may be served by facility j. In some situations a minimum capacity may be required as well, e.g., to guarantee that any opened facility has a minimum level of utilization. When dealing with capacities, the question of demand splitting must also be answered: should all the demand from a given client be satisfied by the same facility, or can the demand be split to different facilities?

For further variations and additional reading on facility location, we direct the reader to some recent reviews and other helpful material:

3.2. NETWORK DESIGN

Location analysis survey	ReVelle and Eiselt [RE05]
Discrete location bibliography	ReVelle, Eiselt, Daskin [RED08]
Review of covering problems	Schilling, Jayaraman, Barkhi [SJB93]
Discrete location textbook	Daskin [D95]
Public sector location problems	Marianov and Serra [MS02]
Discrete location models	Current, Daskin, Schilling [CDS02]

Finally, we note that each of the problems discussed here is $\mathcal{NP}$-hard, though there may be special cases that are solvable in polynomial time.

3.2 Network Design

In network design, the basic problem is to optimally construct a network that enables some kind of flow, and possibly satisfies additional constraints. The nodes are given and the network is constructed from a set of potential edges, or links, each with an associated construction cost.

In [MW84] Magnanti and Wong provide a general problem description of network design that encompasses many variations. Their IP formulation, modified slightly, is given below. The formulation assumes we have a set K of commodities and for each commodity $k \in K$, one unit must be shipped from an origin node $O(k)$ to a destination node $D(k)$. The network should be constructed to minimize the sum of construction and travel costs. The set of nodes is V and the set of links that can be built is L. Each link $ij \in L$ has an associated construction cost c_{ij} and travel cost d_{ij}. The variables y_{ij} are binary variables representing whether or not we build link ij, and the x_{ij}^k are flow variables indicating the flow of commodity k from i to j.

$$\text{Minimize} \quad \sum_{ij \in L} c_{ij} y_{ij} + \sum_{k \in K} \sum_{ij \in L} d_{ij}(x_{ij}^k + x_{ji}^k) \tag{3.9}$$

$$\text{Subject to} \quad \sum_j x_{ji}^k - \sum_l x_{il}^k = \begin{cases} -1 & i = O(k) \\ 1 & i = D(k) \\ 0 & \text{otherwise} \end{cases} \quad \forall k \in K, i \in V \tag{3.10}$$

$$x_{ij}^k \leq y_{ij} \quad \forall k \in K, ij \in L \tag{3.11}$$

$$x_{ji}^k \leq y_{ij} \quad \forall k \in K, ij \in L \tag{3.12}$$

$$x_{ij}^k, x_{ji}^k \geq 0 \quad \forall k \in K, ij \in L \tag{3.13}$$

$$y_{ij} \in \{0,1\} \quad \forall ij \in L$$

Notice that while the links are undirected, the flow has direction. The objective function (3.9) minimizes the sum of construction and travel costs. As in the shortest path IP formulation, we have flow constraints (3.10) and the flow variables need only be greater than zero (3.13). Constraints (3.11) and (3.12) ensure that only built links are used.

The network design work most closely related to the topic of this thesis is the fixed charge network design problem investigated by Balakrishnan, Magnanti, and Wong [BMW89]. This $\mathcal{NP}$-hard problem can be described by the IP formulation above, but in their paper the authors reveal some tricks for tightening the formulation when the origin or destination is the same for one or more commodities. This will be the case in the next section when we look at IP formulations for FLND.

3.2.1 Inverse and Reverse Facility Location

If we consider network design in the context of improving the accessibility of facilities, then the flow we are interested in is that between clients and facilities. Since the structure of the underlying network affects travel from one node to another, manipulating that network can affect facility accessibility. In a problem of this sort, the facilities are already located at fixed sites and we can construct or modify the network to increase accessibility to these facilities.

Using network design to optimize an objective related to clients and facilities is also known as **inverse facility location** or **reverse facility location**, depending on the specifics. In general, in an inverse combinatorial optimization problem, a solution is given and the goal is to modify some problem parameters as little as possible in order to make that solution optimal. In reverse problems, the goal is to improve the given solution as much as possible while not exceeding a given limit (or budget) on the allowed parameter modifications.

In inverse and reverse facility location, the locations of facilities are given and a parameter such as the node or edge weights may be modified. Problems related to network design obviously involve the edge weights. For a survey on inverse location problems, see Heuberger [H04], and for some recent results, Burkard, Pleschiutschnig, and Zhang [BPZ04, BPZ08].

The **reverse p-median problem**, an $\mathcal{NP}$-hard problem, will be of particular interest to us in Chapter 4. First analyzed in 1992 by Berman, Ingco, and Odoni [BIO92], it has the goal of minimizing the total travel cost, and a budget is given for link construction. They considered two different kinds of "construction": In the first, the weights on existing edges in the graph could be decreased, but no new edges added. In this case, which they called network reduction, a linear function for each edge gave the construction cost of reducing the edge's weight by one travel cost unit. Each edge also had a minimum travel cost. The second type of link building involved adding new edges to the graph; existing edges could not be modified. Called network addition, in this case each possible new edge had an associated travel cost and a fixed construction cost.

Other papers have examined reverse p-median problems using network reduction on special classes of graphs [BGH06] or reverse problems with different objectives, such as minimax [BIO94, ZLM00]. Bhadury, Chandrasekharan, and Gewali looked at building a spanning tree network based around a single fixed facility such that the facility is the demand-weighted median of the resulting network [BCG00, BCG03].

3.3 Facility Location–Network Design

Facility location–network design (FLND) involves optimizing objectives related to facilities, and any of the objectives found in facility location may also be an objective in FLND. The means for achieving an objective come from both facility location and network design. That is, in order to optimize access to facilities, we can build both facilities and links. FLND is clearly a generalization of related facility location and network design problems.

In this thesis we consider problems with a median objective, i.e., the primary goal is to minimize the total travel costs. We consider two variations: (1) In the budget version, we have a fixed budget for construction expressed as a constraint and we minimize the total travel costs. (2) In the fixed charge version, we minimize the sum of the construction costs and travel costs. The more we spend on construction, the lower our travel costs will be, and vice versa, so the objective finds an optimal balance between the two. The construction and travel costs are different types of costs, however, so this case assumes we have some kind of equivalency between the two. When studying the problem theoretically we do not need to worry about the cost equivalency, but it becomes an important issue in any application context.

Our problem has the following inputs:

$G = (V, E)$	graph
$K \subseteq V$	set of clients
$J_e \subseteq V$	set of existing facility sites
$J_p \subseteq V$	set of potential facility sites
E	set of existing edges (or links)
L_p	set of potential edges
$a_k, k \in K$	demands at each client
$f_j, j \in J_p$	construction costs for each potential facility
$c_{ij}, ij \in L_p$	construction costs for each potential edge
$d_{ij}, ij \in E \cup L_p$	travel costs on each edge and potential edge

By definition, the set L_p of potential edges may not have duplicates, however, it may contain edges that are also in E. An edge in both E and L_p is an existing edge that has the possibility to be improved. This allows building new links as well as building better versions of existing links. However, to make the problem "cleaner" we prefer not to have any edges in both E and L_p, so we perform a small trick: For any such edge

$ij \in E \cap L_p$, let d_{ij}^E be the travel cost associated with ij in E and $d_{ij}^{L_p}$ be the travel cost associated with ij in L_p (of course $d_{ij}^{L_p} < d_{ij}^E$). Add a new node u that splits up $ij \in E$ so we have two new edges $iu, uj \in E$ each with half the travel cost: $d_{iu} = d_{uj} = d_{ij}^E/2$. The edge $ij \in L_p$ remains with its travel cost $d_{ij} = d_{ij}^{L_p}$. Now we can assume that $E \cap L_p = \emptyset$.

The output of the problem is a subset of the potential facilities J_p and a subset of the potential edges L_p.

Figure 3.1 shows in picture form a sample FLND problem instance (input) and solution (output). This is one of the instances described in detail in Appendix A; the appendix also contains a visual key to the elements of the graph.

According to the objective, we call this problem the **fixed charge facility location–network design problem** (fixed charge FLND) or the **budget facility location–network design problem** (budget FLND).

Facility location–network design problems of this type were first considered in a published work by Melkote in his doctoral thesis from which came the papers [MD01a, MD01b, MD01c, MD98].

In [MD01a] Melkote and Daskin developed an IP formulation for the problem that is based on that of the fixed charge network design problem studied by Balakrishnan, Magnanti, and Wong [BMW89]. Key points that tighten the formulation include scaling the demands to 1 and disaggregating the clients. We present this formulation in detail in the next subsection. For the fixed charge FLND problem, Melkote and Daskin were able to solve problems of size up to 40 nodes and 160 edges efficiently using a standard IP solver. They do a sensitivity analysis for the budget FLND problem on two specific example instances, noting that the amount of budget spent on facilities versus links is affected by the size of the budget and the relative costs of building links and facilities. While the latter is self-evident, in the former case, a larger budget led to more facilities and fewer links being constructed. It should be noted that in all the problems they studied, the initial graph had no links.

The fixed charge FLND problem is $\mathcal{NP}$-hard in the general case, and in [MD01c], Melkote and Daskin developed polynomial time algorithms for two special cases. In both cases, there are no existing links and the set of candidate links forms a tree. The first case involves locating exactly two facilities with no fixed costs. Here the problem amounts to selecting the two facility locations and selecting one link to be excluded from the solution. The second case considers fixed charge FLND, so facilities do have fixed costs and an unknown number are to be located. In this case the authors cleverly translated the problem into a tree-partitioning problem and used an existing algorithm to solve it in $O(n^2)$ time.

In similar studies, the two authors develop IP formulations and present computational results for the capacitated fixed charge FLND problem [MD01b] and for the maximum covering FLND problem (maximum covering objective with demand-specific coverage distances and penalties for uncovered demand) [MD98]. These problems are also $\mathcal{NP}$-hard, but in the latter case they identify two polynomially solvable cases: when the set of possible links forms a tree, and (1) all demand nodes have equal cov-

3.3. FACILITY LOCATION–NETWORK DESIGN

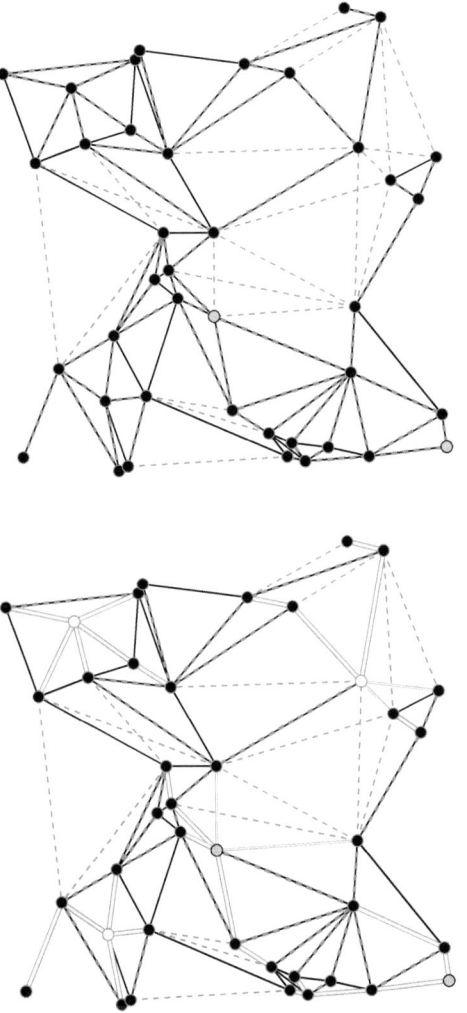

Figure 3.1: The FLND problem instance 222a, and one possible solution.

erage distances, or (2) coverage distances are defined per facility.

There has been very little other research on FLND problems, and none that examines exactly the problem variations that we (and Melkote and Daskin) have studied. Ravi and Sinha [RS06] and Chen and Chen [CC07] have developed approximation algorithms for similar FLND problems with capacitated links, no travel costs, and in the latter case, soft-capacitated facilities (multiple copies of a facility may be built at one location). They call these problems capacitated cable facility location, and soft-capacitated facility location and cable installation, respectively.

Drezner and Wesolowsky consider some variations on network design problems, one of which is essentially an FLND problem where exactly one facility is to be located and the goal is to minimize link construction costs and round-trip travel costs to the facility [DW03]. They implement some metaheuristics for this problem and present results on three 40 node problem instances.

Other researchers have studied FLND-like problems where the network must have a special structure. Current [C88] and Current and Pirkul [CP91] explored the problem of hierarchical network design with transshipment facilities. In this problem, the network must include a primary path between a predetermined source-destination pair as well as a secondary network connecting the remaining nodes to the primary path at sites where transshipment facilities are to be built. The goal is to minimize the costs of building the facilities and network.

Some hub location problems, especially with application in communication networks, go beyond locating hubs and additionally involve the design of a backbone network (among hubs) and/or tributary network (nodes to hubs). Klincewicz provides a review of these sorts of problems [K98].

3.3.1 Disaggregate IP Formulation

In this section we present the IP formulation for FLND developed by Melkote and Daskin in [MD01a], slightly modified. We call this formulation the **disaggregate formulation**, or **D**.

Given the problem inputs as described previously, the demands are first scaled to 1 by introducing client-specific travel costs d_{ij}^k representing the cost of client k traveling link ij: $d_{ij}^k = a_k * d_{ij}$. Now all clients can be treated as if they have demand 1 because the actual demand is incorporated into the travel costs.

As mentioned, the formulation is based on a fixed charge network design formulation as presented in Section 3.2. Instead of commodities, in FLND we have clients. In order to be able to model the problem as pure network design, an additional node s, which we call the **sink** is added. Then to E we add edges js from every existing facility $j \in J_e$ to the sink, and to the potential links L_p we add edges js from every potential facility $j \in J_p$ to the sink, with associated construction cost $c_{js} = f_j$. The travel costs of all the facility-to-sink edges are 0. Now we have a network design problem where the commodities all have different origins, but the same destination: the sink node s. After solving, the flow of the clients/commodities will form a directed spanning tree with s as the root.

3.3. FACILITY LOCATION–NETWORK DESIGN

We use the following variables:

z_j	1 if a facility is built at j 0 otherwise	$\forall j \in J_p$
y_{ij}, y_{ji}	1 if link ij / ji is built 0 otherwise	$\forall ij \in L_p$
x_{ij}^k, x_{ji}^k	fraction of client k traveling i to j / j to i	$\forall k \in K, \forall ij \in E \cup L_p$
w_j^k	fraction of client k served by facility j	$\forall k \in K, \forall j \in J_e \cup J_p$

The w variables represent flow on the facility-to-sink edges and are used, for the sake of clarity, instead of x_{js}^k, $j \in J_e \cup J_p$. Note that in an optimal solution, the x and w variables will be either 0 or 1, meaning a client's demand stays together. For a given link $ij \in L_p$ we have both y_{ij} and y_{ji}. This does not represent one-way links; rather, it is a convenience to mirror the directional flow variables x. In an optimal solution there will be flow in at most one direction on a given link.

Because the solution flow will form a directed, rooted spanning tree, all nodes except the root will have exactly one outbound edge with flow on it. Thus we can make the variable substitutions shown below [MD01a].

Variable	Substitute with
x_{ij}^i	y_{ij}
w_i^i	z_i

Building an outbound link ij from a client i is equivalent to i traveling that link. Building a facility at client node i is equivalent to i using that facility. To put it another way, if we build link ij, client i must travel it, and vice versa. If we build facility i, client i must use it, and vice versa.

Figure 3.2 is a visual aid for understanding the IP formulation variables. Using a very small example, on the left it shows a problem instance, and on the right, the IP formulation's network design graph with variables next to the edges they represent. For example, the edge from node 2 to the sink node s represents a potential facility at 2. The variable z_2, expressing whether or not the facility is built, is associated with this edge. The variables w_2^k, i.e., w_2^1, ($w_2^2 = z_2$), and w_2^3, are also associated with this edge and measure the "flow" on the edge, or the proportion of each client's demand that visits facility 2.

The following IP formulation is for budget FLND. To avoid complicating the formulation more than necessary, we assume below, without loss of generality, that there are no existing edges or facilities ($E = \emptyset, J_e = \emptyset$). This is an easy assumption since we can represent existing elements as "potential" elements whose construction cost happens to

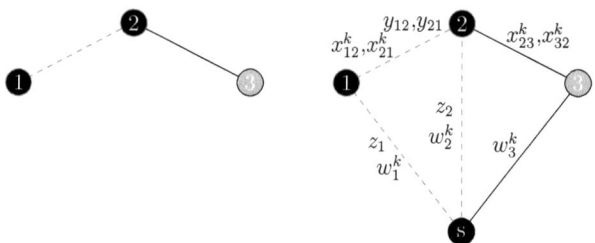

Figure 3.2: IP formulation variables shown on a graph (right) for a simple problem instance (left) involving 3 clients, 1 existing facility (node 3), two potential facilities (nodes 1 and 2), one existing link (2-3), and one potential link (1-2).

be 0. Furthermore we assume that every node is both a client and a potential facility ($V = K = J_p$). If this is not the case, it makes things more complicated to describe but does not change the problem. As a result of these assumptions we can make the variable substitutions discussed above for every node and edge. Additionally, to avoid clutter below we note here that all node indices used, i, j, k, come from the set of nodes V ($= K = J_p$). Finally, we use L to represent the set of all directed edges for which x and y variables exist. So L is formed by taking every $ij \in L_p$ and adding both ij and ji to L.

$$\text{Minimize} \quad \sum_{ij \in L} \sum_{k \neq i} d_{ij}^k x_{ij}^k + \sum_{ij \in L} d_{ij}^i y_{ij} \tag{3.14}$$

$$\text{Subject to} \quad z_i + \sum_j y_{ij} = 1 \quad \forall i \tag{3.15}$$

$$y_{ki} + \sum_{j \neq k} x_{ji}^k = \sum_j x_{ij}^k + w_i^k \quad \forall i, k : i \neq k, ki \in L \tag{3.16}$$

$$\sum_{j \neq k} x_{ji}^k = \sum_j x_{ij}^k + w_i^k \quad \forall i, k : i \neq k, ki \notin L \tag{3.17}$$

$$z_k + \sum_{i \neq k} w_i^k = 1 \quad \forall k \tag{3.18}$$

$$x_{ij}^k \leq y_{ij} \quad \forall ij \in L, k : i \neq k \tag{3.19}$$

$$w_i^k \leq z_i \quad \forall i, k : i \neq k \tag{3.20}$$

$$y_{ij} + y_{ji} \leq 1 \quad \forall ij \in L_p \tag{3.21}$$

$$\sum_{ij \in L} c_{ij} y_{ij} + \sum_i f_i z_i \leq B \tag{3.22}$$

$$x_{ij}^k \geq 0, y_{ij} \in \{0, 1\} \quad \forall ij \in L, k : k \neq i$$

$$w_i^k \geq 0, z_i \in \{0, 1\} \quad \forall i, k : k \neq i$$

3.3. FACILITY LOCATION–NETWORK DESIGN

The objective (3.14) is to minimize the total travel cost, and it is broken into two pieces because when $k = i$ we use y_{ij} instead of x_{ij}^i. Constraints (3.15) through (3.18) can be thought of as the flow constraints. For a given node i, (3.15) states that the demand originating at i (which is 1) will leave i either by being served by a facility at i ($z_i = w_i^i$) or by traveling some link out of i ($y_{ij} = x_{ij}^i$). (3.16) and (3.17) represent the flow passing through node i, stating that the flow in to i must equal the flow out of i. (3.16) is the same as (3.17) except that on the LHS y_{ki} is pulled out for x_{ki}^k when $ki \in L$. The last of the flow constraints, (3.18) states that for all clients k, the demand must find a destination, whether it be at node k itself (z_k) or at some other node i (w_i^k).

Constraints (3.19) and (3.20) ensure that potential links and facilities are not used if they are not built. On any given link, an optimal solution flow will be in only one direction, so we have constraints (3.21). Given a budget of B, the budget constraint (3.22) ensures that the total construction cost of links and facilities does not exceed the budget. The flow variables x_{ij}^k and w_i^k, representing the fraction of client k traveling link ij or being served by facility i respectively, need only be greater than 0.

The fixed charge FLND IP formulation is very closely related. We need only remove the budget constraint (3.22) and add its left hand side to the objective, so that the objective becomes

$$\text{Minimize} \sum_{ij \in L} \sum_{k \neq i} d_{ij}^k x_{ij}^k + \sum_{ij \in L} d_{ij}^i y_{ij} + \sum_{ij \in L} c_{ij} y_{ij} + \sum_i f_i z_i. \qquad (3.23)$$

This objective minimizes the sum of the travel costs and construction costs, finding the optimal balance between the two.

3.3.2 Aggregate IP Formulation

In this section we introduce a new IP formulation for FLND problems. We can reduce the number of variables in the formulation if we aggregate the clients, so that x_{ij} represents the total flow of all demand on ij and w_i represents the total demand served by a facility at i. Then we have the smaller and simpler formulation shown below (using the same notation and assumptions as in the previous formulation), which we call **A**. The constant P represents the entire demand (or population) in the system, i. e.,

$$P = \sum_{k \in K} a_k.$$

$$\text{Minimize} \quad \sum_{ij \in L} d_{ij} x_{ij}$$

$$\text{Subject to} \quad \sum_{j} x_{ji} - \sum_{k} x_{ik} = -a_i \quad \forall i \quad (3.24)$$

$$\sum_{j} w_j = P \quad (3.25)$$

$$x_{ij} \leq P y_{ij} \quad \forall ij \in L \quad (3.26)$$

$$w_j \leq P z_j \quad \forall j \quad (3.27)$$

$$y_{ij} + y_{ji} \leq 1 \quad \forall ij \in L_p \quad (3.28)$$

$$\sum_{ij \in L} c_{ij} y_{ij} + \sum_{j} f_j z_j \leq B \quad (3.29)$$

$$x_{ij}, w_j \geq 0 \quad \forall ij \in L, j$$

$$y_{ij}, z_j \in \{0, 1\} \quad \forall ij \in L, j$$

In this formulation, constraints (3.24) and (3.25) are the flow constraints, with (3.24) stating that every node i should have an outflow of a_i, and (3.25) that all demand must end up at some facility. Constraints (3.26) and (3.27) have the same function as (3.19) and (3.20), ensuring that potential links and facilities are not used if they are not built. In this case we need to add the constant P because it is possible that the entire demand in the system could travel a given link or visit a given facility. The rest of the constraints are as in the previous formulation.

This formulation can be easily changed to a fixed charge formulation in the manner already discussed. Note the ease with which we can accommodate capacitated problems as well: Remove (3.27) and add

$$w_j \geq C_j^{min} z_j \quad \forall j \quad (3.30)$$

$$w_j \leq C_j^{max} z_j \quad \forall j \quad (3.31)$$

where C_j^{min} is the minimum capacity on a facility at j and C_j^{max} is the maximum capacity on a facility at j.

3.3.3 Comparing IP Formulations

Melkote and Daskin [MD01a] and Balakrishnan, Magnanti, and Wong [BMW89] both note that it would be possible to aggregate the clients (or commodities), but disaggregated clients make the formulation tighter, i.e., the solution of the LP relaxation is

3.3. FACILITY LOCATION–NETWORK DESIGN

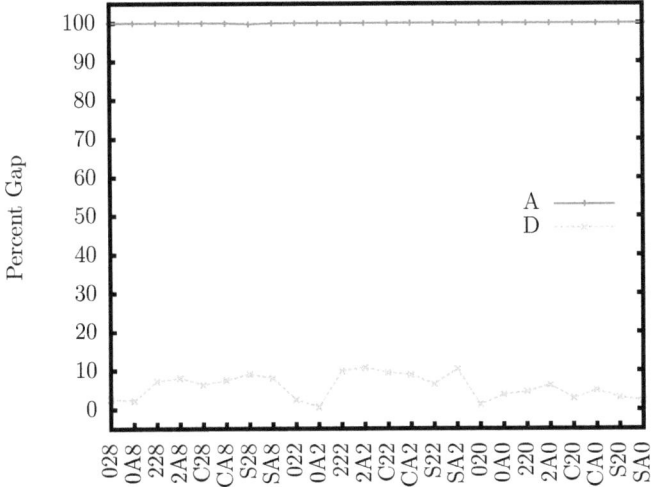

Figure 3.3: Gaps between the LP relaxation solution and optimal solution for the aggregate (A) and disaggregate (D) IP formulations for budget FLND.

closer to optimal. This is certainly true, as can be seen in Figures 3.3 and 3.4, which show the gaps between the LP relaxation solution and optimal solution for the aggregate (A) and disaggregate (D) formulations for budget FLND and fixed charge FLND, respectively. The problem instances along the x axis in each case are the standard test suite used in this thesis and are described in detail in Appendix A, along with the characteristics of the computers on which all tests were run. The problems have 40 nodes and varying other characteristics, including the number and placement of existing and potential links and facilities. The results given for each instance, such as 2.6% for formulation D on instance 028 in Figure 3.3, are actually the average over 3 instances (028a, 028b, 028c) with the same characteristics.

From these graphs we see clearly that the disaggregate IP formulation is to be preferred with respect to the tightness of the LP relaxation. Table 3.1 at the end of the chapter gives these results in tabular format.

We also compared solution times of the two formulations, solving problem instances to optimality using CPLEX 8.1 with all the default settings. Figure 3.5 shows the results, on a logarithmic scale. The problem was solved faster using the aggregated IP formulation A in exactly half the instances, and faster using the disaggregated IP formulation D in half the instances. D was faster on average, never requiring more than an hour, whereas A needed nearly 26 hours in the worst case.

In general, D tended to be faster on the "harder" instances and slower on the "easier" instances, compared with A. This is likely due to the higher overhead when

30   CHAPTER 3. FACILITY LOCATION AND NETWORK DESIGN

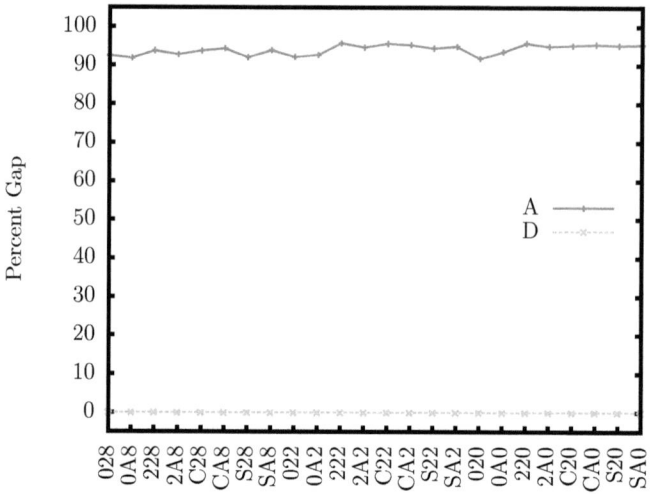

Figure 3.4: Gaps between the LP relaxation solution and optimal solution for the aggregate (A) and disaggregate (D) IP formulations for fixed charge FLND.

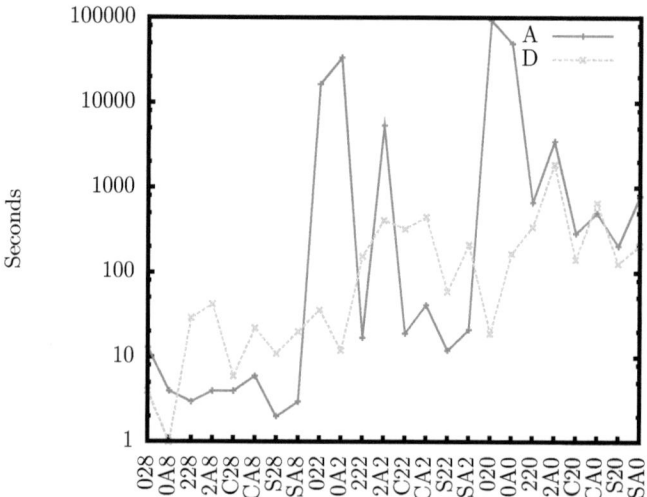

Figure 3.5: Comparison of times for solving to optimality with CPLEX, aggregate (A) and disaggregate (D) IP formulations for budget FLND.

3.3. FACILITY LOCATION–NETWORK DESIGN

using D because it has so many more variables and constraints than A. For a graph with n nodes and m edges, D has $O(mn + n^2)$ variables and $O(mn + n^2)$ constraints, while A has $O(m+n)$ variables and $O(m+n)$ constraints. The size of a CPLEX `.lp` file for the 40-node instances in formulation A ranges from 29 to 76 kilobytes, and in formulation D from 500 kilobytes to 1.7 megabytes. On similar 100 node problems, the file size for A increases to approximately 150 kilobytes and for D to 11 megabytes.

If formulation A could be strengthened so that it has a tight LP relaxation without adding significantly more variables or constraints, it could be a competitive alternative to formulation D. This is the effort we undertake in Chapter 5, Section 5.2. We explore additional classes of inequalities which can be added to the aggregate formulation as cutting planes, with the result that a much better lower bound on the optimal solution is obtained. Though still not tightening the gap as much as the disaggregate model, these cuts do a good job on A and may mitigate its disadvantage in this area.

In the end we conclude that the IP formulation with disaggregated clients is better overall for obtaining good lower bounds on the problem as well as for solving it efficiently by means of an IP solver. However, there may be special cases where formulation A is preferred.

Table 3.1: LP relaxation solution results as percent gap for budget and fixed charge FLND, IP formulations A and D.

Problem	Budget FLND		Fixed Charge FLND	
	A	D	A	D
028	100%	2.6%	92.5%	0%
0A8	100%	2.3%	91.8%	0%
228	100%	7.3%	93.8%	0%
2A8	100%	8.1%	92.7%	0%
C28	100%	6.3%	93.8%	0%
CA8	100%	7.5%	94.4%	0%
S28	99.8%	9.1%	92.1%	0%
SA8	100%	8.0%	93.9%	0%
022	100%	2.5%	92.1%	0%
0A2	100%	0.5%	92.7%	0%
222	100%	9.9%	95.8%	0%
2A2	100%	10.8%	94.7%	0%
C22	100%	9.5%	95.6%	0%
CA2	100%	8.9%	95.3%	0%
S22	100%	6.5%	94.5%	0%
SA2	100%	10.4%	94.9%	0%
020	100%	1.2%	91.8%	0%
0A0	100%	3.8%	93.6%	0%
220	100%	4.6%	95.8%	0%
2A0	100%	6.2%	95.0%	0%
C20	100%	2.9%	95.2%	0%
CA0	100%	5.0%	95.4%	0%
S20	100%	3.0%	95.2%	0%
SA0	100%	2.2%	95.4%	0%

Chapter 4
Upper Bound Approaches: Heuristics

In this chapter we detail each of the heuristics we have developed for FLND. In this endeavor we have concentrated on budget FLND and we present a number of different heuristics for the problem that fall into five families: greedy, custom, basic local search, simulated annealing, and variable neighborhood search. The perspective is a situation where there is an existing network, perhaps with some facilities, and a budget is provided to improve facility access. The heuristics presented assume that the graph is connected by existing edges; no assumption is made regarding existing facilities.

The input to each heuristic is an instance of budget FLND, the data type FLND-inst, which includes the following components:

FLND-inst

$G = (V, E)$	graph
$K \subseteq V$	set of clients
$J_e \subseteq V$	set of existing facility sites
$J_p \subseteq V$	set of potential facility sites
E	set of existing edges (or links)
L_p	set of potential edges
$a_k, k \in K$	demands at each client
$f_j, j \in J_p$	construction costs for each potential facility
$c_{ij}, ij \in L_p$	construction costs for each potential edge
$d_{ij}, ij \in E \cup L_p$	travel costs on each edge and potential edge
B	budget
$M = J_p \cup L_p$	set of potential elements (both facilities and links)
$c_x, x \in M$	construction cost of an element (facility or link)

We have introduced the last two items, M and c_x, to avoid having duplicate pseudocode in some of the heuristics when facilities and links are treated in the same manner. This is a convenience for presentation, and helps make the essential algorithm clear.

It is also helpful to consider a particular feasible solution, data type FLND-sol, with the components shown below. The solution type maintains a graph $G^s = (V^s, E^s)$ which includes an additional node s (which can be thought of as the "sink") with connections to every facility in the solution, including both existing facilities and selected potential facilities, via edges with travel cost 0.

FLND-sol

$inst$	the FLND-inst for which this is a solution
$J^s \subseteq inst.J_p$	selected facilities
$L^s \subseteq inst.L_p$	selected links
s	added "sink" node
$G^s = (V^s, E^s)$	graph with s as described above

In the pseudocode of our heuristics, we may use the following operations on an FLND-sol, sol:

FLND-sol Operations (sol is of type FLND-sol)

sol.init($finst$)	initialize sol with the given FLND-inst (and no selected facilities or links)
sol.add(ele)	add ele, a potential facility or edge, or a set of such, to sol
sol.remove(ele)	remove ele from sol
sol.eles()	return the set of selected elements (both facilities and links) in sol
sol.totCC()	return total construction cost of the elements in sol
sol.facCC()	return total construction cost of the facilities in sol

Additionally, all of the heuristics require an operation that calculates the total travel cost of a solution. We present this as a separate routine and give its pseudocode since it is more complex than the other operations. Algorithm 4.1 shows the function TOTTC, which calculates the total travel cost of a given feasible solution. TOTTC uses DIJKSTRA (Algorithm 2.1) to find the shortest path from every client to s. The len array, received as an output parameter from DIJKSTRA, contains the travel cost of each client to its nearest facility in the solution. In essence, DIJKSTRA builds a shortest path tree rooted at s. Notice that TOTTC returns ∞ if the graph is not connected, i.e., the solution is infeasible. This includes the case where the problem graph, G, is connected, but there is no way to reach the sink, s, because there are no facilities

4.1. GREEDY HEURISTICS

Algorithm 4.1 Calculating total travel cost.

TOTTC(*sol*)
1   *tottc* = 0
2   *connected* = DIJKSTRA(G^s, s, len)
3   **if** *connected*
4   **then for** each client $k \in K$
5   **do** *tottc* += $a_k * len[k]$
6   **else** *tottc* = ∞
7   **return** *tottc*

existing in the problem instance or selected in the solution. TOTTC runs in $O(n^2)$ time where n is the number of nodes in G.

In order to avoid clutter when the context is clear, variables in the pseudocode are not qualified. E. g., instead of writing $sol.G^s$ for the graph G^s that is part of an FLND-sol, *sol*, we just write G^s. In a few heuristics we need to calculate the construction cost of a set (not an FLND-sol) of elements, and for this we use the procedure (pseudocode not shown) CC(S), which returns the total construction cost of the elements in S.

Before presenting the heuristics, we would like to emphasize that the pseudocode given is for the purpose of making clear the essential idea of each algorithm and does not represent an implementation. Therefore we do not handle error cases or include unnecessary code when it would only clutter the pseudocode, although it may be necessary for a robust implementation. The worst case time complexity of each algorithm should be perceivable from the pseudocode. In some cases the reader may notice "inefficiencies" in the code that do not however, affect the time complexity. Rest assured that in our implementations we have attempted to make the code as efficient as possible, while in our presentations of the algorithms, we strive for clarity.

4.1 Greedy Heuristics

As previously stated, we know of no heuristics in the literature for the facility location–network design problems we study. When developing heuristics for a new problem, starting with something simple is often a good idea, so we turn first to greedy heuristics.

A feasible solution to a budget FLND problem consists of a subset of the potential facilities and links, the sum of whose construction costs does not exceed the budget. Our goal is to try to select the subsets that minimize the travel costs of clients to facilities in the resulting graph.

In the greedy additive heuristic, elements (links or facilities) are selected one at a time to add to the solution, until the budget is reached. Each time, the element that produces the greatest improvement in the objective (reducing total travel cost) per unit construction cost is selected. The pseudocode is given in Algorithm 4.2. The input to

Algorithm 4.2 Greedy additive FLND heuristic.

GREEDYADD(*finst*)
1   $cc \leftarrow 0$
2   $sol.\text{init}(\textit{finst})$
3   $basetc \leftarrow \text{TOTTC}(sol)$
4   $S \leftarrow M$
5   **while** $cc < B$ & $S \neq \emptyset$
6   **do** PURGE$(S, B - cc)$
7         $bestRatio \leftarrow 0$
8   **for** each element $x \in S$
9   **do** $sol.\text{add}(x)$
10             $tc \leftarrow \text{TOTTC}(sol)$
11   **if** $(basetc - tc)/c_x > bestRatio$
12   **then** $bestRatio \leftarrow (basetc - tc)/c_x$
13                    $bestEle \leftarrow x$
14                    $besttc \leftarrow tc$
15             $sol.\text{remove}(x)$
16   **if** $bestRatio > 0$
17   **then** $sol.\text{add}(bestEle)$
18               $cc\ += c_{bestEle}$
19               $basetc \leftarrow besttc$
20               $S \leftarrow S \setminus \{bestEle\}$
21   **else** $S \leftarrow \emptyset$
22   **return** sol

PURGE(S, max)
1   **for** each element $x \in S$
2   **do if** $c_x > max$
3   **then** $S \leftarrow S \setminus \{x\}$

4.2. A CUSTOM HEURISTIC

the algorithm is an FLND-inst, *finst*, and the solution created is *sol*, an FLND-sol.

In GREEDYADD, the main loop continues until the budget is depleted or there are no elements remaining that can be added. The set S keeps track of the elements (facilities and links) that may be added to the solution. At the beginning of the loop, S is purged of those elements that are too expensive to add (those that would cause the solution to go over budget). The variable cc keeps track of the total construction cost of the elements added to the solution thus far. Then for each element x in S, the new total travel cost is calculated on a solution with x added. Using this value, line 11 calculates the improvement per unit construction cost and compares it to the best so far. In this way, the best element to add to the solution is found. The algorithm has time complexity $O(n^2m^2)$ where n is the number of nodes in the graph and $m = |M|$ is the number of potential elements that could be added to the solution. (The while loop runs at most m times, the for loop within it also runs at most m times, and TOTTC within the for loop has time complexity $O(n^2)$.)

Another greedy approach is to start with a solution that contains all the potential elements (which is most likely infeasible because of its construction cost) and remove one-by-one those elements whose removal causes the least harm to the objective, until the total construction cost of those elements in the solution falls at or below the budget.

This greedy subtractive approach needs a little twist before it will work properly. Here is why: If we assume that all potential facilities are in the solution, and every client has a facility at its node, then the objective value is 0 and removing any or all of the links will not hurt the objective. Thus in order to make it work properly, we have a first stage where we consider the construction cost of facilities only, and remove facilities from the solution one-by-one until the cost of the solution falls at or below the budget. In the second stage we consider the construction cost of all the elements, and remove elements one-by-one, be they links or facilities, until we are within budget. The pseudocode is given in Algorithm 4.3.

The procedure REDUCE takes a given solution *sol*, a starting construction cost cc, and a set of potential elements S. As long as cc is greater than the budget B, it selects the best element from S to remove from *sol* (the one which least increases the total travel cost, per unit construction cost), and reduces cc by that element's construction cost.

GREEDYSUB starts with a solution containing all the potential links and facilities, and calls REDUCE first with an S containing only the potential facilities and with the total facility construction cost. Thus facilities are removed until the facility construction cost falls below the budget. Then the potential links are added to S, the construction cost is recalculated to be the total construction cost of all elements in the solution, and REDUCE is called again.

4.2 A Custom Heuristic

The greedy heuristics greedily choose the best element, whether facility or link, at each step. However, building links and building facilities have different implications, and in

Algorithm 4.3 Greedy subtractive FLND heuristic.

GREEDYSUB(*finst*)

1   $sol.\text{init}(finst)$
2   $sol.\text{add}(M)$
3   $faccc \leftarrow sol.\text{facCC}()$
4   $S \leftarrow J_p$
5   REDUCE$(sol, faccc, S)$
6   $cc \leftarrow sol.\text{totCC}()$
7   $S \leftarrow S \cup L_p$
8   REDUCE(sol, cc, S)
9   **return** sol

REDUCE(sol, cc, S)

1   $basetc \leftarrow \text{TOTTC}(sol)$
2   **while** $cc > B$
3   **do** $bestRatio \leftarrow \infty$
4   **for** each element $x \in S$
5   **do** $sol.\text{remove}(x)$
6               $tc \leftarrow \text{TOTTC}(sol)$
7   **if** $(tc - basetc)/c_x < bestRatio$
8   **then** $bestRatio \leftarrow (tc - basetc)/c_x$
9                       $bestEle \leftarrow x$
10                      $besttc \leftarrow tc$
11              $sol.\text{add}(x)$
12        $sol.\text{remove}(bestEle)$
13        $cc\ -\!= c_{bestEle}$
14        $basetc \leftarrow besttc$
15        $S \leftarrow S \setminus \{bestEle\}$

4.2. A CUSTOM HEURISTIC

this custom heuristic, CUSTOM, they are treated separately.

Imagine a spectrum of feasible solutions, laid out such that at one end are solutions where the entire budget is spent on links and no facilities are built, and at the other end are solutions where the entire budget is spent on facilities and no links are built. In between are solutions that build some facilities and some links. The idea in CUSTOM is to start at the first end, with no facilities, and methodically proceed to the other end, selecting the best solution found along the way. (If there are no existing facilities in the problem, then we start with one facility.) The steps along the way are determined by the number of facilities in the solution: start with 0, then one facility, then two, up to the number of facilities that may be built if we spent the entire budget on facilities alone.

In this heuristic the subproblems of facility location and network design are solved independently. At each step, a p-median facility location problem is solved first, locating the specified number of facilities, and then with these selected facilities, a network design problem is solved to choose the links with the remaining money. The pseudocode is shown in Algorithm 4.4.

Algorithm 4.4 Custom FLND heuristic.

CUSTOM(*finst*)
```
 1   k ← 0
 2   besttc ← ∞
 3   facCC ← 0
 4   while facCC < B
 5       do sol ← PMED(finst, k)
 6          facCC ← sol.facCC()
 7          if facCC > B
 8              then break
 9          sol ← REVPMED(finst, sol, B − facCC)
10          if TOTTC(sol) < besttc
11              then besttc ← TOTTC(sol)
12                   bestsol ← sol
13          k = k + 1
14   return bestsol
```

The procedure PMED(*finst*,*k*) locates k facilities for the given problem. We wrote this procedure using an efficient implementation of Teitz and Bart's swap-based local search heuristic for the p-median problem [TB68]. Published in 1968, their algorithm is still in use today. Since then, there have been various refinements to the algorithm and improvements to the implementation [W83, RW03], but the basics remain the same. Lately, other more sophisticated p-median heuristics have also been developed, as well as applying metaheuristics to the problem, but clever implementations of Teitz and Bart remain competitive. We use the implementation presented by Resende and

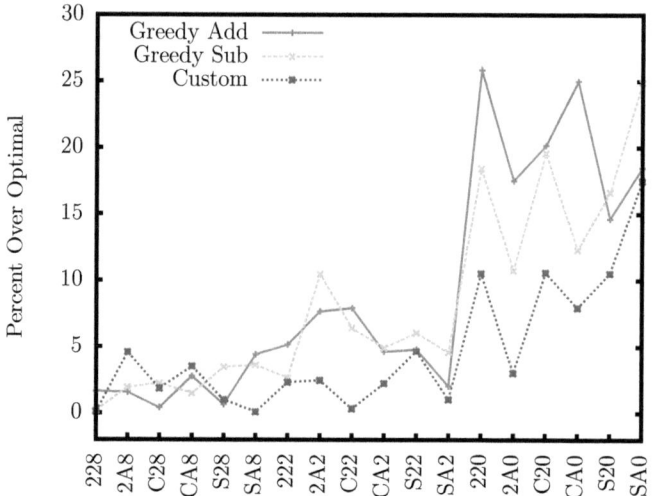

Figure 4.1: Results from greedy additive, greedy subtractive, and custom heuristics, showing percent over optimal of the solution produced.

Werneck [RW03] with worst case running time $O(nm)$ where n is the number of clients and m is the number of potential facilities.

REVPMED(*finst*,*sol*,*cc*) is a heuristic for the reverse p-median problem that assumes the facility set includes any existing facilities in *finst* as well as any selected facilities in *sol*. Links are selected and added to the solution according to a budget of *cc*. This heuristic is based on work by Berman, Ingco, and Odoni [BIO92]. They present a heuristic that allows new edges only, but we extend it to allow for improving existing edges as well. Additionally, their heuristic is faulty in that it overlooks a certain scenario, resulting in miscalculations when this scenario occurs. We have corrected this defect by modifying the heuristic slightly. The time complexity of REVPMED is $O(n^2 m^2)$ where n is the number of nodes in the graph and m is the number of potential links.

Figure 4.1 shows the results of the greedy additive, greedy subtractive, and custom heuristics on the test suite described in Appendix A. The graph shows how far over optimal the results produced by each heuristic were, as a percentage of the optimal solution value. I. e., we define **percent over optimal** of a heuristic solution by the formula

$$\frac{heuristic\_solution\_value - optimal\_solution\_value}{optimal\_solution\_value}.$$

When presenting heuristic results in this chapter, for any heuristic that involves

4.2. A CUSTOM HEURISTIC

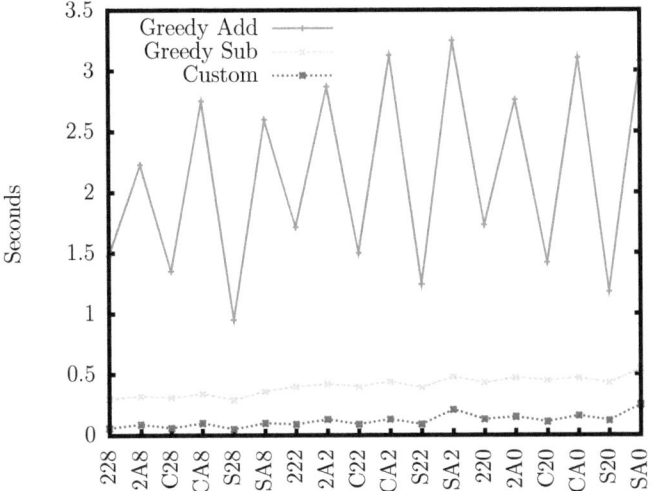

Figure 4.2: Comparison of solving times using the greedy additive, greedy subtractive, and custom heuristics.

some random selections, the best result from 10 runs is used. In this case, the custom heuristic falls into that category because the p-median local search heuristic it uses starts with a random feasible solution.

In terms of solution quality, the custom heuristic performs the best, finding a solution within 4.7% of optimal on average over all the instances. There is no clear winner between the two greedy heuristics, with each performing differently on different instances. The greedy additive heuristic produced a solution within 9.2% of optimal on average and the greedy subtractive within 8.4% on average. All three heuristics had more than one case where the solution they produced was more than 10% over optimal. Table 4.3 at the end of the chapter presents these results in tabular format.

Figure 4.2 compares the running times of the three heuristics, none of which took more than a few seconds to produce a result. All tests were run on a 2.8 GHz machine with 2 GB of RAM, see Appendix A for further details of the test platform. The run time of the greedy additive heuristic clearly depends on the number of potential elements as it runs more quickly for those instances with a '2' as the middle symbol than for those with an 'A': the '2' instances each have 80 potential links, and the 'A' instances have up to 180. See Appendix A for more details on the characteristics of the problem instances.

4.3 Neighborhoods and Neighbor Operators

The remaining heuristics in this chapter use neighborhoods in some way to find a solution. This is a standard notion: a given solution has a neighborhood of similar solutions surrounding it. One way to explore the solution space is to move from neighbor to neighbor via a neighbor operator that is applied to a solution and produces one of its neighbors. We use neighbor operators that produce a random neighbor as well as neighbor operators that produce the best neighbor in a neighborhood.

For budget FLND problems we have developed two different types of neighborhoods: Hamming neighborhoods and step neighborhoods.

4.3.1 Hamming Neighborhoods

When using **Hamming neighborhoods**, we in effect associate a bit with each potential element (link or facility), and a solution is simply a bit string indicating which elements are in the solution. If there are m elements ($|M| = m$), then the bit strings have length m.

Then we define our neighborhoods using Hamming distances. The **Hamming distance** between two bit strings is the number of bits in which they differ. For example, the strings 01101011 and 01111010 are Hamming distance 2 apart: they differ in the 4th and 8th bits. A Hamming distance of 2 means two bit flips, which could be adding 2 elements to a solution (change two 0's to 1's), removing two elements from a solution (change two 1's to 0's), or trading one element for another (change one 0 to 1 and one 1 to 0). If we consider the two given example strings as representing solutions, then the second can be obtained from the first by trading the 8th element for the 4th, i.e., swapping the 8th out and the 4th in.

Using Hamming distances we have a series of expanding neighborhoods to choose from. Given a solution f, we can say that f's neighbors are those solutions of exactly Hamming distance 1 away, or exactly Hamming distance 2 away, etc. In different terminology, f's neighbors are those solutions in Hamming neighborhood 1, Hamming neighborhood 2, etc., of f. Larger Hamming distances produce neighbors that are farther away, or more different, from f. The size of Hamming neighborhood k is $\binom{m}{k} = \frac{m!}{k!(m-k)!}$. So for small values of k relative to m, as k increases, the neighborhoods get bigger as well.

In applying Hamming neighborhoods to budget FLND problems we also need to be aware that a given feasible solution may (and many will) have neighbors that are not feasible because their total construction cost exceeds the budget. In the neighbor operators we develop, we ensure that only feasible solutions are returned.

Algorithm 4.5 shows the pseudocode for a routine that produces a random neighbor in Hamming neighborhood k of a given solution sol. The helper function RAND-COMBO(m, k), whose pseudocode is not shown, returns a random combination of k elements selected from among m. There are $\binom{m}{k}$ possibilities to choose from, so a random number r between 1 and $\binom{m}{k}$ is generated, and the rth combination of k elements, according to a lexicographical ordering, is returned. The procedure for generating the

4.3. NEIGHBORHOODS AND NEIGHBOR OPERATORS

r^{th} combination of k elements from m is described in [M04] and has time complexity $O(m)$. Thus, RANDCOMBO has time complexity $O(m)$.

Algorithm 4.5 Random Hamming neighbor.

RANDHAMMING(sol, k)

1    $cc \leftarrow \infty$
2   **while** $cc > B$
3   **do** $comb \leftarrow$ RANDCOMBO($|M|, k$)
4            $nei \leftarrow$ FLIP($sol, comb$)
5            $cc \leftarrow nei$.totCC()
6   **return** nei

The helper function FLIP($sol, comb$) flips the bits of the elements in sol selected by the elements in the given combination $comb$. For example, suppose we have 8 potential elements, $k = 2$, and $comb = \{2, 6\}$. If sol contains 3 of the 8 potential elements, as indicated by the bit string 10010100 with three 1's out of 8 bits, then FLIP($sol, comb$) produces a solution with elements indicated by the bit string 11010000, i.e., the 2nd and 6th bits are flipped. Assuming k is constant, FLIP runs in constant time.

The while loop in RANDHAMMING ensures that the solution returned is within budget. Ignoring the loop, RANDHAMMING runs with time complexity $O(m)$ (from RANDCOMBO) where $m = |M|$. The closer sol is to the "edge" of the feasible solution space, the more likely random neighbors may not be feasible; however, it is always possible to move "inward" to feasible neighbors, and in reality it shouldn't take that many iterations to do so. In our implementation of the procedure, we put an arbitrary constant limit on the number of iterations on the loop, with an exception thrown if no feasible solution was found. In all our tests, the exception was never thrown.

Algorithm 4.6 shows the pseudocode for a routine that finds and returns the best neighbor (the one with lowest total travel cost) in Hamming neighborhood k of a given solution sol.

Algorithm 4.6 Best Hamming neighbor.

BESTHAMMING(sol, k)

1    $besttc \leftarrow \infty$
2   **for** $comb \leftarrow$ each combination of k elements from $|M|$
3   **do** $nei \leftarrow$ FLIP($sol, comb$)
4   **if** nei.totCC() $\leq B$ & TOTTC(nei) $< besttc$
5   **then** $besttc \leftarrow$ TOTTC(nei)
6                    $bestnei \leftarrow nei$
7   **return** $bestnei$

BESTHAMMING iterates through all possible combinations of k elements from $m = |M|$ to examine every neighbor and find the best feasible neighbor. The iterator used, shown as a for loop in the pseudocode, produces the next combination in constant time assuming constant k. However, there are $\binom{m}{k}$ combinations to check, which is $O(m^k)$ for small k, and calculating the total travel cost for each one takes $O(n^2)$ time, where n is the number of nodes. Thus BESTHAMMING has time complexity $O(m^k n^2)$, or simply $O(m^k)$ if we assume $k > 1$ and m larger than n. Although this is polynomial for constant k, in practical terms, using neighborhoods of larger k can take much longer than using neighborhoods of small k. In our heuristics we do not use a k larger than 3 when finding the best Hamming neighbor.

4.3.2 Step Neighborhoods

In **step neighborhoods**, the neighborhood of a given feasible solution f includes all those solutions that differ from f in at most *step* money's worth of elements (assuming construction costs are measured in monetary units). For example, suppose the total construction cost of the elements in solution f is 600 monetary units. Then if $step = 100$, the neighbors of f include those solutions that differ from f in up to 100 monetary units worth of elements.

In contrast to Hamming neighborhoods, which were based on a certain number of elements moving in or out of a solution, step neighborhoods concern a certain value of elements being swapped in and out of a solution. With varying construction costs for each element, Hamming neighbors can have widely varying total construction costs from each other. Step neighbors, on the other hand, will have approximately the same construction costs (subject to the range of individual element costs), but possibly widely varying numbers of elements from each other. For example, imagine an "expensive" facility being swapped for multiple "inexpensive" links.

Step neighborhoods are not as nice to work with because the construction costs may not be round numbers and it may not be easy or possible to find a grouping of elements whose construction costs add up to a given step. Additionally, it is not clear how to enumerate all the neighbors in a step neighborhood. For these reasons we do not use step neighborhoods in heuristics that require finding the best neighbor in a given neighborhood.

We do, however, have a routine that generates a random neighbor in a given step neighborhood, shown in Algorithm 4.7. While it may not draw equally from all parts of the step neighbor space, it still proved a useful neighbor operator. Using step neighborhoods we can, in practice, have a much greater "reach" than we have with Hamming neighborhoods. When limited to small k, the Hamming neighbor operators give solutions that are fairly close neighbors. With step neighborhoods we can handle a large step, allowing us to create neighborhoods with solutions that are more different than the given solution.

Much of the work in the RANDSTEP procedure is done by the helper function RANDELES(S,*maxcc*), which randomly selects a subset of elements from S, whose total construction cost is not more than *maxcc*. The function RAND(S) simply returns a

4.4. LOCAL SEARCH

Algorithm 4.7 Random step neighbor.

RANDSTEP(*sol*, *step*)
1   nei.init($sol.inst$)
2    $elesOut \leftarrow$ RANDELES(sol.eles(), $step$)
3    $ccIn \leftarrow B - (sol.\text{totCC}() - \text{CC}(elesOut))$
4    $elesIn \leftarrow$ RANDELES($M \setminus sol$.eles(), $ccIn$)
5   nei.add($elesIn \cup sol$.eles() $\setminus elesOut$)
6   **return** nei

RANDELES(S, $maxcc$)
1    $cc \leftarrow 0$
2    $R \leftarrow \emptyset$
3   **while** $cc \leq maxcc$
4   **do** $e \leftarrow$ RAND(S)
5            $R \leftarrow R \cup \{e\}$
6            $cc \leftarrow cc + c_e$
7            $S \leftarrow S \setminus \{e\}$
8    $R \leftarrow R \setminus \{e\}$
9   **return** R

single random element selected from S. RANDELES works by selecting random elements from S one by one until the construction cost of the selected elements exceeds *maxcc*, and the last selected element is not included in the returned set. In order not to select the same element twice, once an element is selected, it is removed from the local copy of S. If we assume that removing an element takes $O(|S|)$ time, then RANDELES has time complexity $O(|S|^2)$, and RANDSTEP has time complexity $O(m^2)$ where $m = |M|$ is the number of potential elements.

4.4 Local Search

The FLND local search heuristic is a standard local search that starts from a given solution and searches for its best neighbor, moving to the neighbor found and repeating the process until no more improvement is possible. Because we must find the best neighbor, this heuristic is implemented with only Hamming neighborhoods.

The initial solution to the given problem instance is generated randomly according to the procedure shown in Algorithm 4.8. RANDINITSOL has a little bit of logic to it: First it randomly adds facilities to the solution, until the budget is reached. Then it randomly adds links with any remaining money, the assumption being that links typically cost less than facilities. In tests, this approach worked better than adding elements completely randomly. In most of our test instances there are a greater number

Algorithm 4.8 Random initial solution.

RANDINITSOL(*finst*)
1   *sol*.init(*finst*)
2   *facs* ← RANDELES(J_p, B)
3   *cc* ← CC(*facs*)
4   *links* ← RANDELES($L_p, B - cc$)
5   *sol*.add(*facs* ∪ *links*)
6   **return** *sol*

---

of possible links that can be added than facilities (as in a graph there can be more edges than nodes) and if no preference is given to facilities, the initial solutions too often end up with all or mostly links. An additional intuitive reason for the preference given to facilities is that facilities have potentially more "power" than links: a facility at a given node reduces the travel cost to 0 for demand at that node, but a link always has a positive travel cost. In Chapter 7 we explore this relationship in more detail in a case study.

RANDINITSOL is used to generate initial solutions for heuristics in upcoming sections as well. It uses the RANDELES procedure introduced in the previous section and has time complexity $O(m^2)$, $m = |M|$.

The local search algorithm, shown in Algorithm 4.9, performs a local search starting from the given initial solution. As can be seen in the pseudocode, neighborhoods of Hamming distance 2 are used, allowing two additions, two subtractions, or one swap between neighbors. Each iteration of the local search loop has time complexity $O(m^2)$; it is difficult to know how many iterations may be required. In the next section we present results, including run times, of the basic local search heuristic along with the simulated annealing heuristics.

Algorithm 4.9 Local search heuristic.

LOCALSEARCH(*finst, sol*)
1   *nei* ← BESTHAMMING(*sol*, 2)
2   *profit* ← TOTTC(*sol*) − TOTTC(*nei*)
3   **while** *profit* > 0
4   **do** *sol* ← *nei*
5   *nei* ← BESTHAMMING(*sol*, 2)
6   *profit* ← TOTTC(*sol*) − TOTTC(*nei*)
7   **return** *sol*

4.5 Simulated Annealing

One of the disadvantages of the basic local search is that it can get stuck at a local minimum with no way to get out. Thus a number of heuristics have been developed that are variations on local search and provide some means of escaping local minima. Simulated annealing is one of these.

The idea behind simulated annealing comes from the physical process of annealing, in which a solid (usually a metal or glass) is heated to a given temperature and then slowly cooled in order to achieve an optimal crystal structure.

As an algorithm, we have a parameter representing the temperature, which has some initial high value and is decreased according to a temperature reduction function. Looping continues until the temperature falls below a predetermined point, or some other stopping condition is met. In each iteration through the loop a random neighbor of the current solution is selected. If the neighbor is better, it becomes the current solution. If the neighbor is not better, it becomes the current solution anyway according to a probability that is calculated based on the temperature. For a temperature t, the commonly used probability is $e^{-\frac{\text{cost}(neighbor)-\text{cost}(solution)}{t}}$, where $cost$ is the quantity we want to minimize, the objective value. At higher temperatures, it is more likely that a neighboring solution will be accepted despite being worse than the current solution. In this way, the solution jumps around a lot initially, and as the temperature decreases, it settles down. For a more detailed explanation of simulated annealing, see, for example, [H03].

In applying simulated annealing to budget FLND, we use both step and Hamming neighborhoods since only random (and not best) neighbors need be generated. We tried Hamming 2, 3, and 4 neighborhoods, and the results were nearly the same, so we settled on Hamming 2. The step we use in step neighborhoods is equal to the maximum construction cost of a single element, thus ensuring that any element can be swapped in or out.

The temperature reduction function we use is $f(t) = t * 0.99$. Initially we want to allow all neighbor transitions, regardless of whether the neighbor is better or not, thus we set the initial temperature to the maximum difference in objective value between two neighboring solutions. We estimate this value by generating a fixed number of random neighbors of the initial solution and taking the maximum difference found. We run 100 iterations at each temperature value before applying the temperature reduction function, and we terminate when the temperature falls below 0.5. These parameters can be customized; the values given here were determined after a large number of test runs using different values.

The FLND simulated annealing heuristic is shown in Algorithm 4.10. We use a randomly generated feasible solution as the initial solution passed into the routine. Though not shown in the pseudocode, we keep track of the best solution found throughout the process. Since a solution may be abandoned for a neighbor that is not as good, it would otherwise be possible to end up with a final solution that is not as good as some previously visited solution.

The pseudocode shown uses Hamming neighborhoods; the step neighborhoods version, SIMANN-STEP, differs only in that it makes a call to RANDSTEP instead of RANDHAMMING. The worst case time complexity of each iteration through the loop is dominated by the call to $O(n^2)$ TOTTC in the Hamming version and $O(m^2)$ RAND-STEP in the step version, where n is the number of nodes and $m = |M|$ is the number of potential elements.

Algorithm 4.10 Simulated annealing heuristic.

SIMANN-HAM(*finst*, *sol*)
1    $t \leftarrow$ initial temperature
2    $cnt \leftarrow 0$
3   **while** $t > 0.5$
4   **do** $nei \leftarrow$ RANDHAMMING(sol, 2)
5   **if** TOTTC(nei) < TOTTC(sol)
6   **then** $sol \leftarrow nei$
7   **else** $r \leftarrow$ random real number between 0 and 1 inclusive
8   **if** $r < e^{-\frac{\text{TOTTC}(nei) - \text{TOTTC}(sol)}{t}}$
9   **then** $sol \leftarrow nei$
10   cnt++
11   **if** $cnt \geq 100$
12   **then** $t \leftarrow t * 0.99$
13                    $cnt \leftarrow 0$
14   **return** sol

Figure 4.3 shows the quality of solutions produced by the local search heuristic from the previous section and the two simulated annealing heuristics. Of the three, the local search heuristic performed best for most instances, averaging 2.5% over optimal across all the instances. Simulated annealing with step neighborhoods was a close second, giving solutions that averaged 2.6% over optimal. Simulated annealing with Hamming neighborhoods didn't do as well, averaging 7.9% over optimal, and producing solutions more than 20% over optimal in three cases. Table 4.3 at the end of the chapter presents these results in tabular format.

Figure 4.4 shows the run times of the three heuristics. These heuristics take much longer than the few seconds of the greedy and custom heuristics, but still less than 2 minutes for the most part on our test platform (see Appendix A). As we also saw with the greedy additive heuristic, the local search run times depend heavily on the number of potential elements that can be added to the solution. This makes sense because at each iteration a search is done of every combination of 2 elements (for Hamming distance 2) from the set of potential elements.

We also tried using a temperature reduction factor of 0.9999 in the simulated annealing heuristics, which we would expect to take much longer but also to produce better results. In this case, each run of the heuristic took two to three hours on our test platform, much longer than any of the other heuristics in this chapter. The results

4.5. SIMULATED ANNEALING

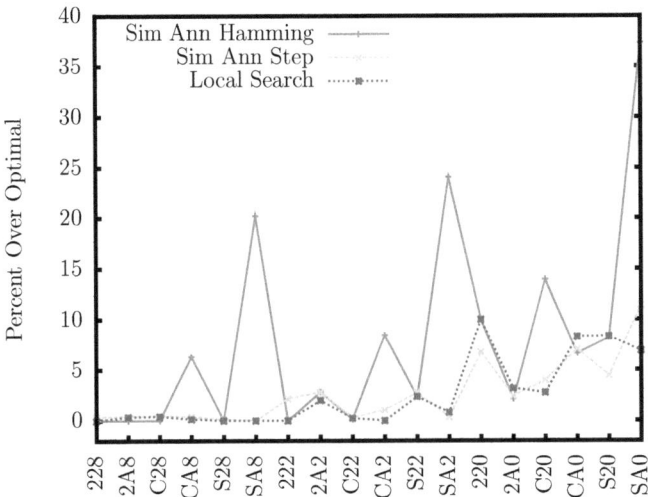

Figure 4.3: Results from local search and simulated annealing heuristics, showing percent over optimal of the solutions produced.

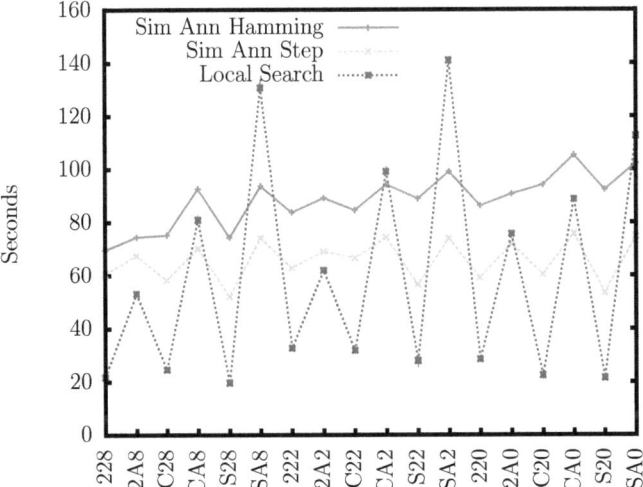

Figure 4.4: Comparison of solving times using the local search and simulated annealing heuristics.

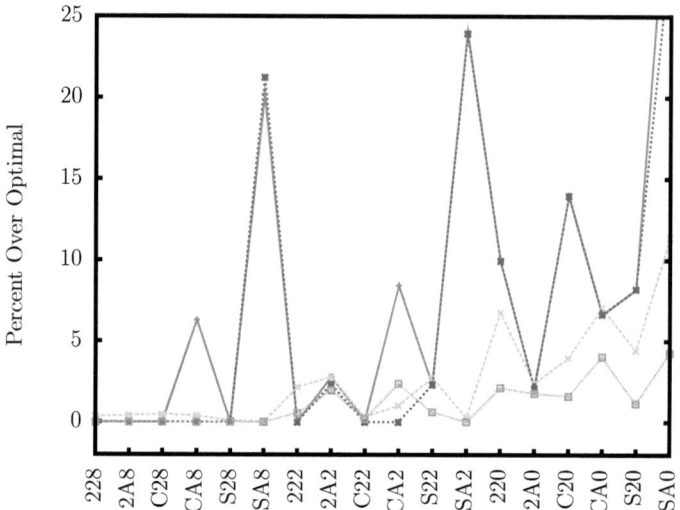

Figure 4.5: Comparison of simulated annealing heuristic results using $f(t) = t * 0.99$ versus $f(t) = t * 0.9999$ temperature reduction function.

obtained, shown in Figure 4.5, were somewhat better than with temperature reduction factor 0.99, averaging 6.7% (as opposed to 7.9%) over optimal for the Hamming version and 1.2% (as opposed to 2.6%) over optimal for the step version.

4.6 Variable Neighborhood Search Heuristics

Like simulated annealing, variable neighborhood search is based on a local search, with added mechanisms to avoid getting stuck in local minima. The idea is to use various different neighborhoods rather than a single kind of neighborhood. When a local minimum is reached, switch to a different neighborhood to try to escape. Any series of neighborhoods may be used, but the intent is that the neighborhoods be expanding. Then if the heuristic gets stuck in one neighborhood, the next neighborhood will give access to neighbors that are farther away, with the hope of jumping out of the local minimum.

Variable neighborhood search (VNS) is a relatively more recent metaheuristic, introduced by Hansen and Mladenović in 1997 [MH97a]. They have developed a family of heuristics based on the idea of variable neighborhoods. For more detailed descrip-

4.6. VARIABLE NEIGHBORHOOD SEARCH HEURISTICS

tions see [HM01, HM03, HMP01]; we will only present those variants that we have applied to budget FLND, namely, basic variable neighborhood search, reduced variable neighborhood search, and variable neighborhood descent.

Algorithm 4.11 describes the basic outline of all three of the VNS heuristics. The function NEIGHBOR in line 4 is a placeholder for a specific neighbor function: In reduced variable neighborhood search and basic VNS, a random neighbor in the kth neighborhood is obtained, e.g., by calling RANDHAMMING. In variable neighborhood descent, the best neighbor in the kth neighborhood is found. Line 5, the local search, is present only in basic VNS.

The main loop continues as long as improved solutions continue to be found, or alternatively, until a limit on the number of iterations with no improvement is reached. Neighborhoods are successively explored, starting with the first, or innermost, neighborhood, $k = 1$, and proceeding until the last, k_{max}. At each neighborhood, a neighboring solution is generated and if it is better, it is kept and k is optionally reset to 1. If no better solution is found, k is increased and the algorithm moves on to the next neighborhood.

Algorithm 4.11 Variable neighborhood search outline.

VNS(*finst*, *sol*)
1   **while** improvement continues
2   **do** $k \leftarrow 1$
3   **while** $k < k_{max}$
4   **do** $nei \leftarrow$ NEIGHBOR(sol, k)
5   [$nei \leftarrow$ LOCALSEARCH(*finst*, *nei*)]
6   **if** TOTTC(nei) < TOTTC(sol)
7   **then** $sol \leftarrow nei$
8   [$k \leftarrow 1$]
9   **else** $k \leftarrow k + 1$
10 **return** sol

In each of the variable neighborhood search heuristics that we have implemented, we use a randomly generated solution (RANDINITSOL, Algorithm 4.8) as the initial solution. Because these algorithms continue as long as improvement is made, the time complexity is difficult to determine.

4.6.1 Basic Variable Neighborhood Search

In the basic variable neighborhood search, at each iteration a random neighbor in the kth neighborhood is generated and a local search is performed starting with this neighbor. The local search can be any local search heuristic and does not need to use the same neighborhoods as the variable neighborhood search. In our case, we use the local search described in section 4.4.

Algorithm 4.12 shows the pseudocode for BASICVNS-HAM, the basic variable neighborhood search using Hamming neighborhoods. The series of neighborhoods used is determined by k: neighborhood k uses Hamming distance k to find neighbors. We use a k_{max} of 4 and continue until there have been 10 iterations with no improvement. Given our problem sizes, the k_{max} of 4 is the largest we can go and be able to store values up to $\binom{m}{k_{max}}$ in a standard long integer. The number of iterations with no improvement, 10, was selected somewhat arbitrarily, but with the intent that good solutions not be missed while at the same time the heuristic not take unreasonably long (no more than an hour) to run.

In the version that uses step neighborhoods, BASICVNS-STEP (not shown), neighborhood 1 has a step equal to the maximum construction cost of an element, $maxcc$, and successive neighborhoods go up in step by half that amount. That is, the step for neighborhood k is $maxcc + (0.5 * maxcc * (k-1))$. With step neighborhoods, neighborhood k is farther away from the current solution than with Hamming neighborhoods, and in this case we use a k_{max} of 3.

Algorithm 4.12 Basic variable neighborhood search heuristic.

BASICVNS-HAM(*finst, sol*)
1   *noImprove* ← 0
2   **while** *noImprove* < 10
3   **do** k ← 1
4   *improved* ← FALSE
5   **while** $k < 4$
6   **do** *nei* ← RANDHAMMING(*sol, k*)
7   *nei* ← LOCALSEARCH(*finst, nei*)
8   **if** TOTTC(*nei*) < TOTTC(*sol*)
9   **then** *sol* ← *nei*
10   k ← 1
11   *improved* ← TRUE
12   **else** k ← $k + 1$
13   **if** *improved*
14   **then** *noImprove* ← 0
15   **else** *noImprove*++
16 **return** *sol*

Figure 4.6 graphs the solution quality of the Hamming and step basic VNS heuristics. They both find the optimal solution for many of the "easier" problems, but clearly the step version does better overall than the Hamming version, averaging only 0.6% over optimal across the problem instances, to Hamming's 2.1%.

In Figure 4.7 we see the solve times. In contrast with the previous heuristics presented, these heuristics have run times in the multiple minutes, even surpassing an hour in two cases. The problem instance SA0, which goes off the chart, required nearly

4.6. VARIABLE NEIGHBORHOOD SEARCH HEURISTICS

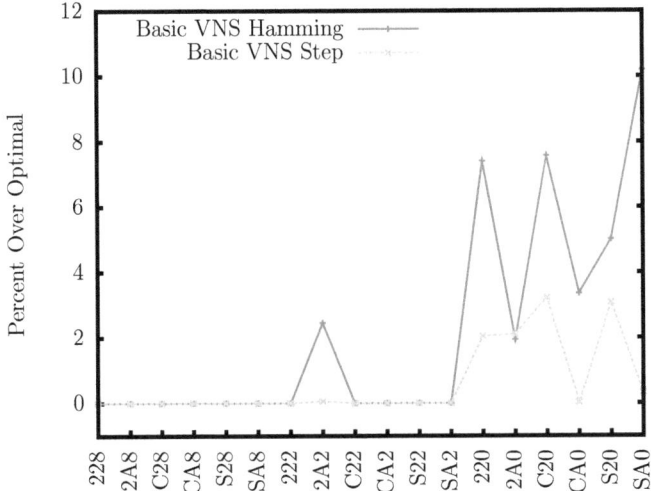

Figure 4.6: Results from basic variable neighborhood search heuristics, showing percent over optimal of the solutions produced.

8000 seconds, or 133 minutes, on average (across the three a, b, and c instances) for BASICVNS-STEP to produce a solution. This lengthy run time, however, is worthwhile in the sense that these are more difficult instances, and BASICVNS-STEP produced far better solutions that the other heuristics.

The step version of basic VNS generally has much longer running times than the Hamming version, despite using fewer neighborhoods. An investigation revealed that the Hamming and step versions of basic VNS go through approximately the same number of iterations. Thus they make approximately the same number of calls to the local search routine, which is where the bulk of the run time is spent. However, the local search itself goes through about five times as many iterations in step VNS as in Hamming VNS. (The same local search procedure is used in both step VNS and Hamming VNS.) What this shows is that the random step neighbors that are generated as the starting point for the local search are significantly farther from a local minimum than the random Hamming neighbors.

4.6.2 Reduced Variable Neighborhood Search

Reduced variable neighborhood search (RVNS) is reduced in the sense that it only selects random neighbors; the local search step is not present. It has a very fast running time in comparison to basic VNS, but tends to produce solutions that are not as good. The pseudocode for RVNS is shown in Algorithm 4.13. We use a k_{max} of

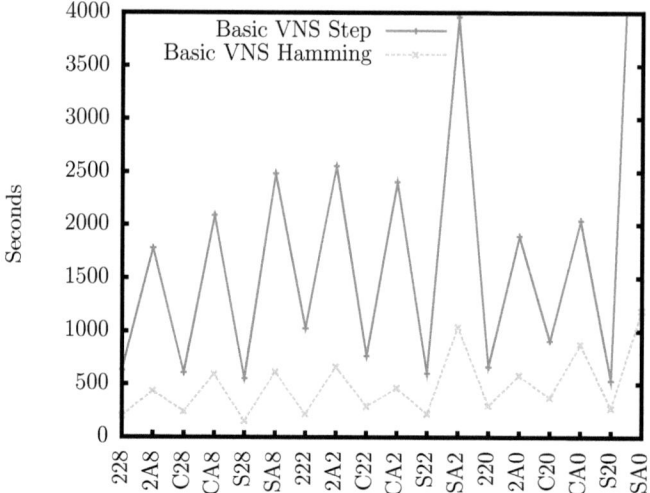

Figure 4.7: Comparison of solving times using basic variable neighborhood search.

4 for both Hamming and step neighborhoods and continue until there have been 100 iterations without any improvement. The series of Hamming and step neighborhoods are determined in the same manner as in the basic VNS heuristic.

The results of the two RVNS heuristics are shown in Figure 4.8. Interestingly, RVNS-HAM, averaging 4.9% over optimal, does much better than RVNS-STEP with 11.2% over optimal on average. This contrasts with basic VNS as well as the two simulated annealing heuristics, in which step neighborhoods were the decided winner. Clearly the choice of neighbor operator is important, and different operators may work better with different heuristics.

The run times of the RVNS heuristics are shown in Figure 4.9. Like the greedy and custom heuristics, RVNS is fast, with run times no more than a few seconds on our test platform.

4.6.3 Variable Neighborhood Descent

While reduced VNS generates only random neighbors, variable neighborhood descent (VND) generates only best neighbors. VND is the natural extension of a basic local search to using multiple neighborhoods. It performs a local search on the innermost neighborhood, and when a local minimum is reached, it moves on to the next neighborhood, remaining in that neighborhood until no more improvement is possible, then moving on to the next, and so on.

Since we need to find the best neighbor in this heuristic, we have only one version,

4.6. VARIABLE NEIGHBORHOOD SEARCH HEURISTICS

Algorithm 4.13 Reduced variable neighborhood search heuristic.

RVNS-HAM(*finst, sol*)
1   *noImprove* ← 0
2   **while** *noImprove* < 100
3   **do** $k \leftarrow 1$
4   *improved* ← FALSE
5   **while** $k < 4$
6   **do** *nei* ← RANDHAMMING(*sol*, k)
7   **if** TOTTC(*nei*) < TOTTC(*sol*)
8   **then** *sol* ← *nei*
9                $k \leftarrow 1$
10   *improved* ← TRUE
11   **else** $k \leftarrow k + 1$
12   **if** *improved*
13   **then** *noImprove* ← 0
14   **else** *noImprove*++
15   **return** *sol*

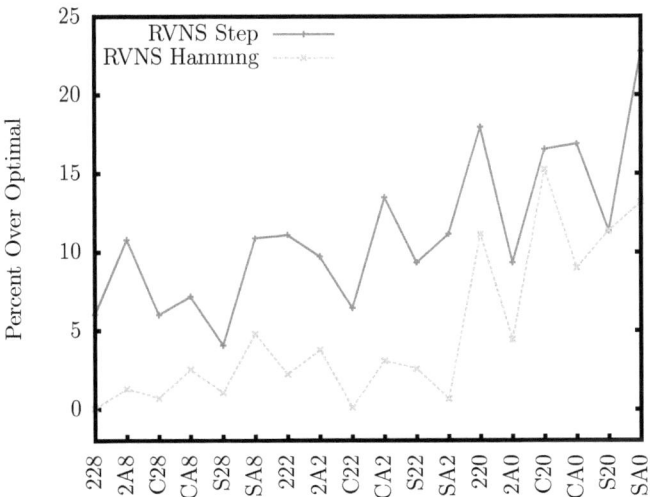

Figure 4.8: Results from reduced variable neighborhood search heuristics, showing percent over optimal of the solutions produced.

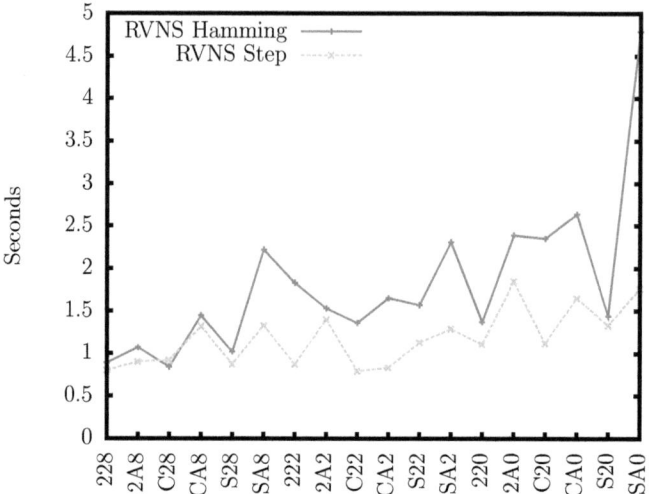

Figure 4.9: Comparison of solving times using reduced variable neighborhood search.

using Hamming neighborhoods. We use a k_{max} of 3. A larger k_{max} could give greater possibilities for finding a better solution, but given the size of our problem instances, 3 was the highest value that would keep running times "reasonable." The pseudocode is shown in Algorithm 4.14.

The outer while loop that runs as long as there is improvement may not be necessary, depending on the neighbor operator. Once a cycle through the neighborhoods 1 to k_{max} is complete, there is no better neighbor in the k_{max} neighborhood. It may be unlikely that there is a better neighbor in the $k = 1$ or any $k < k_{max}$ neighborhood.

Figure 4.10 shows the VND solution quality results along with the basic VNS results. In terms of both solution quality and run time, VND falls between the basic VNS Hamming and step heuristics, averaging 2.0% over optimal, just slightly better than BASICVNS-HAM. Performance on individual problem instances varies greatly among the three heuristics.

In Figure 4.11, all five VNS heuristics are shown together, and one can clearly see that the basic VNS heuristic with step neighborhoods produces the best solutions. Table 4.4 at the end of the chapter presents these results in tabular format.

4.7 Comparison and Discussion

Table 4.1 summarizes the results from each of the heuristics we have presented for budget FLND problems. The average solution quality over all problem instances, as

4.7. COMPARISON AND DISCUSSION

Algorithm 4.14 Variable neighborhood descent heuristic.

VND(*finst, sol*)
1   *improvement* ← TRUE
2   **while** *improvement*
3   **do** $k \leftarrow 1$
4   *improvement* ← FALSE
5   **while** $k < 3$
6   **do** *nei* ← BESTHAMMING(*sol, k*)
7   **if** TOTTC(*nei*) < TOTTC(*sol*)
8   **then** *sol* ← *nei*
9   *improvement* ← TRUE
10   **else** $k \leftarrow k + 1$
11 **return** *sol*

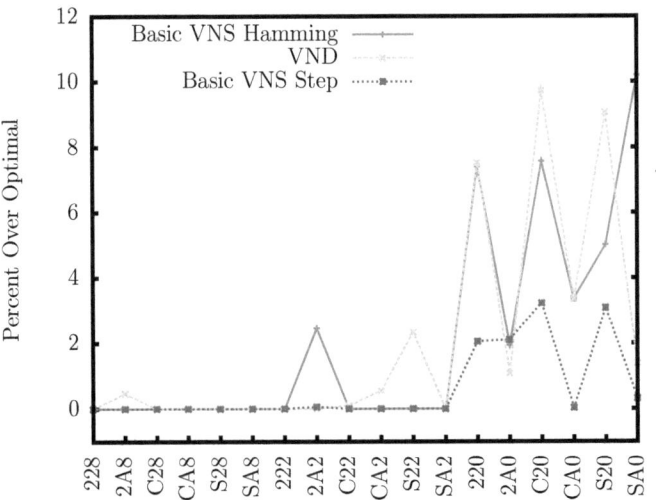

Figure 4.10: Results from variable neighborhood descent along with basic VNS, showing percent over optimal of the solutions produced.

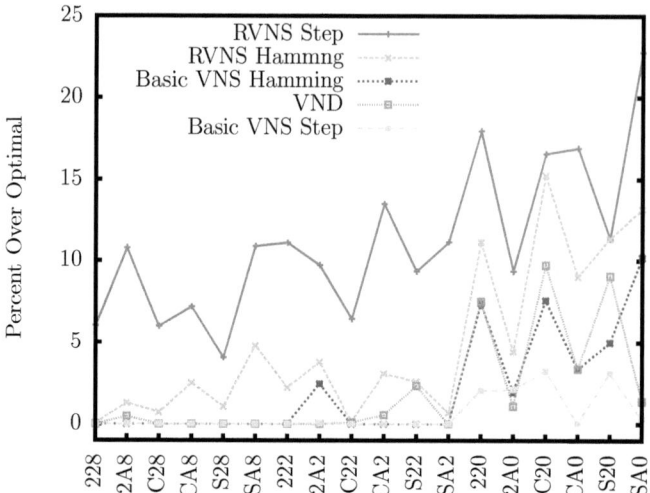

Figure 4.11: Results from all variable neighborhood search heuristics, showing percent over optimal of the solutions produced.

percentage over the optimal solution, is given, along with the worst performance for each heuristic. The heuristics are ranked from best average to worst average. Basic VNS with step neighborhoods is the winning heuristic with the best average case as well as worst case performance in terms of solution quality. Figure 4.12, though somewhat crowded, shows the solution quality of all heuristics on each problem instance on a single graph.

The neighbor operator used plays an important role in the performance of those heuristics that are based on neighborhoods. In general, the heuristics using step neighborhoods do better than their counterparts that use Hamming neighborhoods, with RVNS being the exception. The local search and VND heuristics, however, which have only Hamming versions, also do relatively quite well. Interesting future work could be to develop alternate step neighbor generators and alternate neighbor operators altogether.

Run time can be a consequential factor in selecting a heuristic, and the one delivering the highest quality results may not be the best overall for a given situation if the time requirements are too high. Table 4.2 shows the average and longest run times of each heuristic in seconds on our test platform. While the exact run times are less important as they can vary greatly depending on the platform, we can see how the heuristics compare to each other. In the table they are ranked from fastest to slowest.

Figure 4.13 shows the run times of all heuristics plotted on one graph with a logarithmic time scale. Here we can see three groupings of the heuristics in terms of time:

4.7. COMPARISON AND DISCUSSION

Table 4.1: Comparison of average and worst case solution quality (percent over optimal) for all heuristics.

Heuristic	Average	Worst Case
Basic VNS Step	0.6%	3.2%
VND	2.0%	9.7%
Basic VNS Hamming	2.1%	10.2%
Local Search	2.5%	10.0%
Sim Ann Step	2.6%	11.4%
Custom	4.7%	17.5%
RVNS Hamming	4.9%	15.3%
Sim Ann Hamming	7.9%	37.4%
Greedy Sub	8.4%	24.9%
Greedy Add	9.2%	25.9%
RVNS Step	11.2%	22.8%

Table 4.2: Comparison of average and longest solving times for all heuristics, shown in seconds.

Heuristic	Average	Longest
Custom	0	0
Greedy Sub	0	1
RVNS Step	1	2
Greedy Add	2	3
RVNS Hamming	2	5
Local Search	60	141
Sim Ann Step	66	76
Sim Ann Hamming	88	105
Basic VNS Hamming	484	1192
VND	765	3593
Basic VNS Step	1859	7992

CHAPTER 4. UPPER BOUND APPROACHES: HEURISTICS

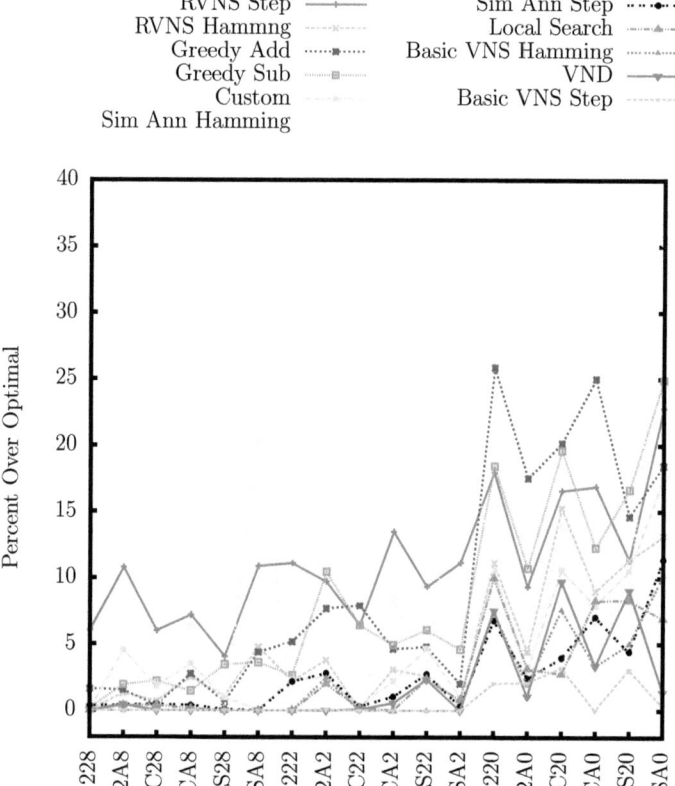

Figure 4.12: Results from all heuristics shown on one graph, percent over optimal of the solutions produced.

4.7. COMPARISON AND DISCUSSION

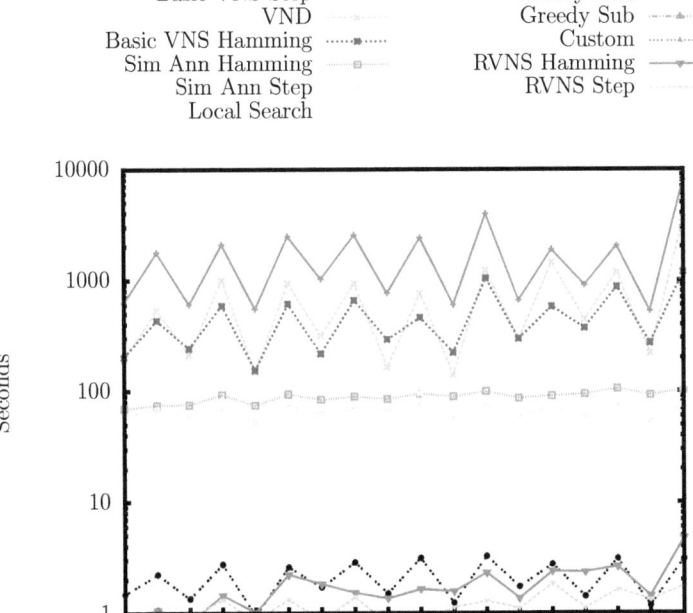

Figure 4.13: Comparison of solving times of all heuristics shown on one graph.

those that take at most a few seconds (greedy, custom, and RVNS), those with run times from multiple seconds up to a couple of minutes (simulated annealing and local search), and those requiring multiple minutes up to significant portions of an hour, or more (basic VNS and VND).

In the fast group, the custom heuristic has the best solution quality; in the middle group, the local search; and in the slowest group, step basic VNS, which is the slowest overall and also produces the highest quality results overall.

Table 4.3: Results from greedy, custom, local search, and simulated annealing heuristics, percent over optimal.

Problem	Greedy Add	Greedy Sub	Custom	Local Search	Sim Ann Step	Sim Ann Hamming
228	1.6%	0.2%	0.1%	0.0%	0.4%	0.0%
2A8	1.6%	2.0%	4.6%	0.4%	0.4%	0.0%
C28	0.4%	2.2%	1.9%	0.4%	0.5%	0.0%
CA8	2.8%	1.5%	3.5%	0.2%	0.4%	6.3%
S28	0.6%	3.5%	1.0%	0.0%	0.1%	0.0%
SA8	4.4%	3.6%	0.1%	0.0%	0.0%	20.2%
222	5.2%	2.6%	2.3%	0.0%	2.2%	0.0%
2A2	7.7%	10.5%	2.5%	2.0%	2.8%	2.8%
C22	7.9%	6.4%	0.3%	0.2%	0.3%	0.1%
CA2	4.6%	5.0%	2.2%	0.0%	1.1%	8.4%
S22	4.8%	6.1%	4.7%	2.4%	2.8%	2.3%
SA2	2.0%	4.6%	1.0%	0.8%	0.3%	24.1%
220	25.9%	18.4%	10.5%	10.0%	6.8%	10.0%
2A0	17.5%	10.7%	3.0%	3.2%	2.4%	2.1%
C20	20.2%	19.6%	10.6%	2.8%	4.0%	14.0%
CA0	25.0%	12.3%	7.9%	8.3%	7.1%	6.6%
S20	14.6%	16.7%	10.5%	8.3%	4.4%	8.2%
SA0	18.5%	24.9%	17.5%	6.9%	11.4%	37.4%

Table 4.4: Results from variable neighborhood search heuristics, percent over optimal.

Problem	Basic VNS Hamming	Basic VNS Step	VND	RVNS Hamming	RVNS Step
228	0.0%	0.0%	0.0%	0.1%	6.0%
2A8	0.0%	0.0%	0.5%	1.3%	10.8%
C28	0.0%	0.0%	0.0%	0.7%	6.0%
CA8	0.0%	0.0%	0.0%	2.5%	7.2%
S28	0.0%	0.0%	0.0%	1.1%	4.1%
SA8	0.0%	0.0%	0.0%	4.8%	10.9%
222	0.0%	0.0%	0.0%	2.2%	11.1%
2A2	2.5%	0.1%	0.0%	3.8%	9.7%
C22	0.0%	0.0%	0.1%	0.1%	6.5%
CA2	0.0%	0.0%	0.6%	3.1%	13.5%
S22	0.0%	0.0%	2.3%	2.6%	9.4%
SA2	0.0%	0.0%	0.0%	0.7%	11.2%
220	7.4%	2.1%	7.5%	11.2%	18.0%
2A0	1.9%	2.1%	1.1%	4.4%	9.4%
C20	7.6%	3.2%	9.7%	15.3%	16.6%
CA0	3.4%	0.0%	3.4%	9.0%	16.9%
S20	5.0%	3.1%	9.1%	11.4%	11.4%
SA0	10.2%	0.3%	1.4%	13.2%	22.8%

Chapter 5

Lower Bound Approaches

The heuristics presented in the last chapter provide methods for finding an upper bound on the optimal solution to an FLND problem. In this chapter we explore approaches to finding a good lower bound on the optimal solution to an FLND problem.

Recall the two IP formulations presented in Chapter 3: the one introduced by Melkote and Daskin [MD01a] in which clients are disaggregated, called **D**; and the one we introduced in which clients are aggregated, called **A**. We saw that the lower bounds obtained by solving the LP relaxation were much better for D as compared with A. Table 5.1 summarizes the information presented in various figures from Chapter 3. It shows the average gap between the LP relaxation solution and the optimal solution over all problem instances in the test suite, for budget FLND and fixed charge FLND. The 100% gap for formulation A on budget FLND problems means that the objective value when solving the LP relaxation is 0.

Simply put, the goal in this chapter is to reduce those gaps. We concentrate on budget FLND since it is the "harder" problem in terms of the gaps, as demonstrated in Table 5.1. We examine each IP formulation separately and develop additional valid inequalities and related separation routines that improve the lower bounds. At the end of the chapter we compare the best bounds of each formulation.

Table 5.1: Summary of LP relaxation gaps of A and D: averages over all instances in the test suite.

	Budget	Fixed Charge
D	5.8%	0%
A	100%	94%

5.1 Improving the LP Relaxation of the Disaggregate IP

The disaggregate IP formulation is already fairly tight, but there is room for improvement. The inequalities we developed for the aggregate IP (which occurred first chronologically, though is presented in the next section) do not help with the disaggregate IP. However, by examining fractional solutions to small problems we were able to come up with some valid inequalities that cut off some of these fractional solutions.

5.1.1 Knapsack Cuts

We discovered that the fractional solutions to the LP relaxation of D often violated knapsack inequalities relative to the budget. For example, in one specific 4-node problem instance, the fractional solution built two facilities and one link completely (variable value 1) and 0.829 of a third facility. Given the budget and construction costs, however, it would only be possible to build three of the four elements. Thus we could add an inequality such as

$$z_1 + z_3 + z_4 + (y_{2,3} + y_{3,2}) \leq 3$$

where z_1, z_3, z_4, and $(y_{2,3} + y_{3,2})$ represent whether or not each of the four elements are built. This is the basic idea of the **knapsack cuts** for budget FLND. At this point, the reader is encouraged to review formulation D, presented in Section 3.3.1, as we use the same variables and notation in the current discussion. Recall in particular that binary variables z_i represent whether or not a facility is built at node i and binary variables y_{ij} represent whether or not a link is built between nodes i and j.

To generate all possible knapsack inequalities is not practical or desirable: if M is the set of potential facilities and links, it would involve examining every set in the power set of M, of which there are $2^{|M|}$. While it may be possible with some tricks to avoid having to examine every set, we know of no method that is efficient when $|M|$ is large. A better strategy is to try to find a maximally violated cut.

Our knapsack cut separation routine works based on a fractional solution and selects a subset of the potential links and facilities to base the cut on. A knapsack cut is generated involving only those z and y variables that represent selected elements. The basic structure of the routine is shown in Algorithm 5.1.

We tried four different strategies for selecting the z and y variables, and one was the clear winner. We also implemented two different ways of finding a knapsack-style cut on the selected variables, one with good results, and the other with results not quite as good, but using less time and memory.

The variable selection strategies we tried were the following:

1. **Vv**: Select the n variables with the highest value (integer or fractional) in the fractional solution.

2. **Cc**: Select the n variables with highest associated construction cost.

5.1. IMPROVING THE LP RELAXATION OF D

Algorithm 5.1 Knapsack separation routine.

KNAPSACKSEPARATION(*fracsol*)
1   $zy \leftarrow$ SELECTZYS(*fracsol*)
2   $cut \leftarrow$ MAKECUT(zy)
3   **if** *cut* is violated by *fracsol*
4   **then** add *cut*

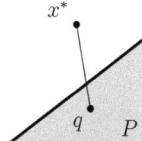

Figure 5.1: The target cut is the facet of polytope P that is crossed by a line segment connecting the fractional solution x^* with a point q inside P.

3. **Vvcc**: Select the n variables with the highest product of variable value (integer or fractional) multiplied by associated construction cost.

4. **Rand**: Randomly select n variables from among those with positive value (integer or fractional).

Strategy Vvcc produced the best cuts, i.e., most violated and leading to greatest gap closure. This is also a good strategy intuitively because it measures the amount that each element currently contributes toward the budget (in the current fractional solution), and we would expect a cut involving these variables to be most violated.

5.1.1.1 Target Cut Method

Once the variables are selected, we generate a knapsack cut (the call to MAKECUT in Algorithm 5.1) via either the **target cut method** or the **ones plus method**. The target cut method uses target cuts as described by Buchheim, Liers, and Oswald [BLO08], which are similar to local cuts as given by Cook et al. [ABCC01].

In the target cut method, shown in Algorithm 5.2, we first generate all feasible solutions (those within budget) on the selected variables. This is done by considering every set in $\mathcal{P}(X)$, the power set of X, where X is the set of selected variables. If the sum of the construction costs of the selected elements (i.e., the elements associated with the selected variables) in the subset is within the budget, then the solution is feasible.

Assuming n variables are selected, i.e., $|X| = n$, the feasible solutions can be thought of as points in n-dimensional space. These points are collected in set F in the algorithm pseudocode, and are passed, along with the fractional solution, to the target cut procedure TCUT by Buchheim, Liers, and Oswald. Figure 5.1 depicts the cut that is found and returned by their procedure. They consider the polytope, P, formed by the convex hull of the feasible solution points, and the fractional solution x^*. The cut returned is the facet hit by a line segment connecting x^* to some point q inside the polytope. In our case, we use the center of mass of the polytope for q. They solve an LP to obtain this facet. For a more detailed description, see their paper [BLO08]. Whenever the fractional solution is outside the polytope, a violated cut is found.

Algorithm 5.2 Target cuts method of making a knapsack cut.

TARGETCUT($zy, fracsol$)
1   $F \leftarrow \emptyset$
2   **for** each set $S \in \mathcal{P}(zy)$
3   **do if** $\text{CC}(S) \leq B$
4   **then** $F \leftarrow F \cup \{S\}$
5   $cut \leftarrow \text{TCUT}(fracsol, F)$
6   **return** cut

Since we need to examine the elements of the power set of the set of selected variables, there are practical limitations on the number of variables we can select. In our implementation, we limit the number of selected variables to at most 19, the largest number that our test platform could handle for the problems in our test suite. See Appendix A for a description of the test suite and test platform.

While the most intuitive knapsack cuts, such as the four-variable example given earlier, have coefficients no larger than 1, this is not true of many of the cuts generated by the target cut routine. The cuts do tend to have a structure, with similar coefficients for variables whose associated construction costs are similar, and higher construction costs correlated with larger coefficients. The following is an actual target cut returned on one of the test suite problems (problem 220a):

$$10z_3 + 9z_{31} + 9z_{21} + 9z_{29} + 9z_{27} + 9z_{12} + 12z_{40} + 10z_{24} + 14z_{11} + 9z_7$$
$$+ 3y_{18,3} + 10z_{36} + 9z_{22} + y_{28,3} + 10z_{19} + y_{13,23} + y_{32,23} \leq 52$$

5.1.1.2 Ones Plus Method

The ones plus method is an attempt to generate knapsack style cuts in a more efficient manner, in terms of both time and memory. Before introducing the ones plus method, we introduce its predecessor ONESCUT, shown in Algorithm 5.3, which is used as a starting point for ones plus cuts.

ONESCUT builds a valid knapsack cut with coefficients no greater than 1. It loops through the selected variables in the order given, with the assumption that earlier

5.1. IMPROVING THE LP RELAXATION OF D

Algorithm 5.3 Ones cut, knapsack cut with all 1 coefficients.

ONESCUT(zy)
1   Initialize cut with 0 coefficients
2    $ccSum \leftarrow 0$
3    $S \leftarrow \emptyset$
4    $phase1 \leftarrow$ TRUE
5   **for** each $x \in zy$
6   **do if** $phase1$
7   **then**   ▷ Phase 1
8                $ccSum \leftarrow ccSum + \text{CC}(x)$
9                $cut.coeff[x] \leftarrow 1$
10               $S \leftarrow S \cup x$
11   **if** $ccSum > B$
12   **then** $cut.rhs \leftarrow |S| - 1$
13                        $phase1 \leftarrow$ FALSE
14   **else**   ▷ Phase 2
15               $newcut \leftarrow cut$
16               $newcut.coeff[x] \leftarrow 1$
17   **if** ONESVALID($newcut$)
18   **then** $cut.coeff[x] \leftarrow 1$
19   **return** cut

---

variables should be more likely to go into a cut than later variables. In our implementation, the variables are ordered based on their selection by strategy Vvcc. There are two distinct phases during the loop: In phase one, each variable is added to the cut with coefficient 1 until the total construction cost of the variables in the cut exceeds the budget. At this point the RHS is set and the algorithm moves on to phase two, which continues in the same loop. If there are n variables that have been added at the end of phase 1, then the value of the RHS is set to $n-1$. At this stage, we clearly have a valid knapsack cut: Since the n elements with 1 coefficient go over budget, no more than $n-1$ can be in a feasible solution.

In phase two we try to add more variables to the cut without changing the RHS while maintaining the cut's validity. Continuing in the loop, the remaining variables are examined and added to the cut with coefficient 1 if doing so does not make the cut invalid. The validity test is performed in line 17 with the call to ONESVALID, whose pseudocode is not shown. We can add a variable to the cut and it remains valid as long as the total construction cost of the $rhs+1$ variables in the cut with lowest individual construction costs, is still over budget. In this case, checking validity can be done in linear time. The entire ONESCUT procedure has time complexity $O(n^2)$, where $n = |zy|$ is the number of selected variables.

The ones plus method, shown in Algorithm 5.4, starts with a ones cut and tries to

Algorithm 5.4 Ones plus method of making a knapsack cut.

ONESPLUS(zy)
1    $cut \leftarrow$ ONESCUT(zy)
2    $r \leftarrow 0$
3   **while** $r \leq |zy|$
4   **do** $newcut \leftarrow cut$
5           $newcut\,.\,rhs$ ++
6           $newcut\,.\,coeff\,[zy[r]]$ ++
7   **if** INCCOEFFS($newcut$)
8   **then** $cut \leftarrow newcut$
9                    $r \leftarrow 0$
10   **else** r ++
11 **return** cut

INCCOEFFS(cut)
1    $incd \leftarrow$ FALSE
2   **for** each $x \in zy$
3   **do** $cut\,.\,coeff\,[x]$ ++
4   **if** POSSBVALID(cut)
5   **then** $incd \leftarrow$ TRUE
6   **else** $cut\,.\,coeff\,[x]$ − −
7   **if** $incd$
8   **then if** !VALID(cut)
9   **then** $incd \leftarrow$ FALSE
10 **return** $incd$

5.1. IMPROVING THE LP RELAXATION OF D

increase the coefficients and the RHS further, such that the violation of the cut by the fractional solution is increased.

ONESPLUS loops through each selected variable. During one iteration, it increments the RHS and the coefficient of the current variable, creating a new valid cut. This new cut itself will not be any more helpful, but the increase of the RHS may allow other coefficients to be increased as well. This is attempted in the procedure INCCOEFFS. If successful, we keep the cut and go back to the first variable in the list. If unsuccessful, we revert back to the original cut and move on to the next variable. If necessary, provisions for avoiding an infinite loop may be added, such as a limit on the RHS.

INCCOEFFS increases the coefficient of each selected variable by at most 1. It loops through the variables, incrementing the coefficient, and keeping the change only if the cut remains possibly valid, as determined by the call to POSSBVALID (pseudocode not shown). The check for possible validity is a heuristic with linear time complexity that quickly detects some invalid cuts, but may return true for others. If POSSBVALID returns false, the cut is definitely invalid, and if it returns true, the cut is only possibly valid. POSSBVALID works in a similar fashion to ONESVALID, but instead of looking at the $rhs +1$ elements with smallest construction cost, it looks at the $rhs +1$ coefficient-weighted elements with smallest division of construction cost by coefficient. If the sum of the construction costs of these elements is within budget, then the cut is invalid. If not, it might be valid.

After the loop completes, INCCOEFFS checks for final validity by calling VALID, which is an exact check, returning true if and only if the given cut is valid. VALID works by looping over the power set of the set of variables in the cut with positive coefficients. There need exist only one subset with the following property to make the cut invalid: the total construction cost associated with the variables is within (less than or equal to) the budget *and* the sum of their coefficients is greater than the RHS. The former condition indicates the existence of a feasible solution where all the variables in the subset are 1, and the latter condition indicates that this solution would be cut off by the given cut, and thus the cut is invalid. Due to its exponential run time, VALID is not used in the loop.

As a tweak in ONESPLUS, though not shown in the pseudocode, we add the following in our implementation: After the main while loop completes, we force a coefficient increase of 1 on the first variable and the RHS and repeat the whole while loop again. This was found to sometimes produce better cuts. As in our target cuts method, we limit the number of variables to at most 19 in the ones plus implementation. Finally, it should be noted that we keep track of the most violated cut encountered throughout the process, and that is the one returned at the end.

5.1.2 Results

In Section 3.3 we examined the gaps between optimal solutions and lower bounds provided by solving the LP relaxations of IP formulations A and D. The lower curve in Figure 3.3 showed gaps for formulation D on budget FLND problems, ranging from 0.5% to just under 11%. To improve these lower bounds, we adopt the cutting plane

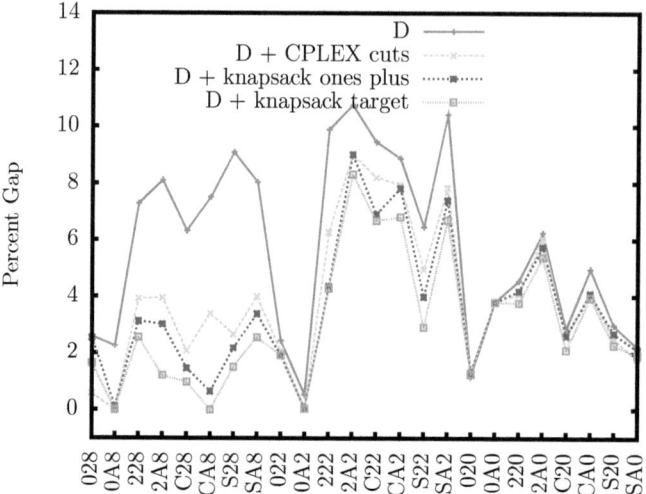

Figure 5.2: Comparison of lower bounds obtained from solving the root node using the disaggregate IP plus various cuts, measured in percentage gap between the lower bound and optimal solution.

approach: we take the LP relaxation solution and employ our separation routine to generate cuts, which we then add to the formulation, and solve it again. This is done repeatedly until no more useful cuts are found. In fact, what we are doing is solving the root node (only) in a branch-and-cut tree.

In the implementation, we take advantage of the CPLEX branch-and-cut procedure, allowing it to manage most of the branch-and-cut details. We plug in our separation routine via a cut callback and solve only the root node.

Figure 5.2 shows the lower bounds obtained by solving the disaggregate LP relaxation (D) alone, adding the generic cuts provided in CPLEX, adding knapsack cuts using the ones plus method, and adding knapsack cuts using the target cut method. Knapsack cuts using the target cut method performs the best, giving the best lower bound for all problem instances except two (028 and SA0), and even obtaining the optimal solution in a small number of cases. Table 5.5 at the end of the chapter gives these results in tabular form.

In tests not shown, we also tried including both ones plus knapsack cuts and target knapsack cuts, but this did not improve on the target knapsack cuts alone.

Table 5.2 summarizes the results across all problem instances. The knapsack target cuts close the gap from the LP relaxation lower bound an additional 48% and clearly outperform the CPLEX cuts as well as the knapsack ones plus cuts. The knapsack ones plus cuts perform a little better than the CPLEX cuts.

5.2. IMPROVING THE LP RELAXATION OF A

Table 5.2: Summary of root node lower bound gap results using formulation D plus cuts. The last column shows the average gap closure achieved by adding cuts to the LP relaxation.

	Low	Average	High	Gap Closure
D	0.53%	5.79%	10.27%	
D + CPLEX cuts	0%	3.89%	9.03%	32.8%
D + knapsack ones plus	0.05%	3.52%	9.01%	39.2%
D + knapsack target	0%	3.02%	8.31%	47.8%

When solving on our test platform (see Appendix A for details) the run times using CPLEX cuts averaged about 30 seconds; using knapsack ones plus cuts, just under 6 minutes; and using knapsack target cuts, around 70 minutes.

5.2 Improving the LP Relaxation of the Aggregate IP

We now turn our attention to improving the lower bounds produced by the LP relaxation of the aggregate IP formulation, A. As noted previously, Melkote and Daskin [MD01a] as well as Balakrishnan, Magnanti, and Wong [BMW89] mention that disaggregating the clients produces a much tighter IP formulation than aggregated clients, and they do not explore an aggregate IP. However, formulation A has the advantage of using fewer variables than formulation D: $O(n+m)$ compared to $O(nm+n^2)$, where n is the number of nodes and m the number of edges. For this reason, we thought it worthwhile to consider this formulation further, and in particular to attempt to strengthen it.

In this section we introduce some cuts that can be added to A's LP relaxation to greatly improve the poor lower bounds. In the end we will see that the lower bounds produced in this manner are still not as good as those from the LP relaxation of formulation D. The cuts, however, are a nice development for formulation A, and could have greater value revealed by future efforts.

Table 5.1 at the beginning of the chapter showed that solving the LP relaxation of formulation A on our test problems produced gaps averaging 100% for budget FLND and 94% for fixed charge FLND. To understand why the gaps are so large, consider the constraints that ensure potential links and facilities are not used unless they are built:

$$x_{ij} \leq P y_{ij} \quad \forall ij \in L$$
$$w_j \leq P z_j \quad \forall j$$

Because all the clients are aggregated, we have a large constant, P, which is the total population or demand in the system. Thus the values of the y and z variables can typically remain very small to accommodate the amount of demand flowing on a given link or visiting a given facility. This in turn means only a very small amount of money must be spent to allow the demand to reach a facility. The typical fractional solution builds just enough of a facility at every node to accommodate the demand at that node. Thus the travel costs are 0, and in budget FLND problems, the objective is 0 and the gap is 100%. In fixed charge FLND problems, the objective value consists only of the small amount of money spent building the fractional facilities.

5.2.1 Subset Cuts

If the main problem with the formulation is the big P, one way to counteract that is to look at a smaller subset of nodes in the graph, and the total demand of only the nodes in that subset. Given a problem instance with graph $G = (V, E)$, and a subset $R \subseteq V$ with total demand $a_R = \sum_{k \in R} a_k$, we can make the statement

$$\text{(demand leaving } R\text{)} + \text{(demand served in } R\text{)} \geq a_R.$$

This is not a strict equality because there may be demand from nodes not in R both leaving R (after entering) and being served by a facility in R.

To create a mathematical inequality from this statement, we could write the following:

$$\sum_{i \in R} \sum_{j \in V \setminus R} x_{ij} + \sum_{i \in R} a_R z_i \geq a_R \tag{5.1}$$

For simplicity of exposition, we are assuming that every node is a client and potential facility. (Whether the edges are existing or potential is irrelevant to these inequalities– every edge has associated flow variables.)

The first term on the left hand side of (5.1) captures the flow out of R, i.e., demand traveling on edges going out of R.

The second term is an upper bound on the demand from R that is served within R. Since facilities do not have capacities, if any node in R has a facility built at it, up to the entire demand in R could visit that facility. Of course $a_R z_i$ may be an overestimation of the demand from R attending a facility at i. A different, and in some cases tighter, upper bound is the following:

$$a_i z_i + \left(\sum_{k \in R} x_{ki} \right) z_i \tag{5.2}$$

This states that the demand from R attending a facility at i will be the demand at i itself plus any demand flowing into i from other nodes k in R. By itself, this term does not account for demand from R that may leave R and then return to node i via an edge that originates outside R. However, using this term in our inequality is valid because any demand that leaves R will be captured by the first term in (5.1). In order

5.2. IMPROVING THE LP RELAXATION OF A

to make (5.2) linear, we can set the second z_i to 1 since we are dealing with an upper bound. Then we have an inequality that looks like this:

$$\sum_{i \in R} \sum_{j \in V \setminus R} x_{ij} + \sum_{i \in R} \left(a_i z_i + \sum_{k \in R} x_{ki} \right) \geq a_R \qquad (5.3)$$

It turns out that sometimes $a_R z_i$ is smaller than $a_i z_i + \sum_{k \in R} x_{ki}$ and sometimes vice versa. Thus in our separation routine for these **subset cuts**, we pick the smaller of the two based on the fractional solution and add inequality (5.1) or (5.3) accordingly.

Algorithm 5.5 shows our subset separation routine. We begin by picking one or more promising subsets, then we make a subset cut, (5.1) or (5.3), for each selected subset, adding the violated cuts.

Algorithm 5.5 Subset separation routine.

SUBSETSEPARATION(*fracsol*)
1 $S \leftarrow$ PICKSUBSETS(*fracsol*)
2 *cuts* $\leftarrow$ MAKECUTS(S, *fracsol*)
3 **for** each *cut* in *cuts*
4   **do if** *cut* is violated by *fracsol*
5   **then** add *cut*

For large problems, it is not possible to generate a cut for every possible subset, so we tried a number of different strategies for selecting subsets, of which we mention three: One strategy generated all subsets of small size, up to five nodes. A second strategy used a simulated annealing heuristic to find a subset producing a cut with violation as large as possible. The final strategy generated random connected subsets of various sizes up to half the number of nodes. Of all the strategies we tried, the random connected subsets performed the best, so it is the one we used.

Our PICKSUBSETS routine (pseudocode not shown) generates n subsets each of sizes 1 to $n/2$ nodes, where n is the number of nodes in the graph. Each subset is generated randomly by selecting a random starting node and then adding additional nodes up to the appropriate number. Additional nodes are added by randomly selecting a neighboring node of one of the nodes already in the subset. In this way the subset remains connected. Prior tests showed that random connected subsets generally produce better subset cuts than completely random subsets.

The MAKECUTS routine (pseudocode not shown) simply checks whether $a_R z_i$ or $a_i z_i + \sum_{k \in R} x_{ki}$ is smaller in the fractional solution and creates cut (5.1) or (5.3), respectively.

Note that in SUBSETSEPARATION, the subsets picked are not dependent on the fractional solution, and each time separation is performed we create multiple random subset cuts as described, adding only the violated ones. After a number of iterations of subset separation and re-solving the LP, further generated subset cuts are not useful.

5.2.2 Similar Inequalities in the Literature

There have been similar inequalities to our subset inequalities mentioned in the literature and used for the purpose of strengthening an LP relaxation. Ravi and Sinha [RS06] study a problem somewhat similar to ours (as mentioned in Chapter 3), the capacitated cable facility location problem. Their IP formulation for the problem includes constraints on every subset S of the nodes of the graph. The constraint states that S must contain at least one open facility or have at least one cable leaving the set. The authors call these "connectivity constraints" and note that they strengthen the LP relaxation.

Barahona [B96] studies the capacitated network loading problem, a multicommodity network design problem, and solves a relaxation based on "cut inequalities" in his solution approach. These inequalities come from the so-called cut condition, a necessary condition for the existence of a multicommodity network flow. Multiple units of capacitated links may be built in this problem, and the cut condition states that for any node subset S, there must exist enough link capacity leaving S to accommodate the demand with sources in S and destinations outside of S. The inequality derived from this condition is clear: at least as much link capacity leaving S must be built as the total demand with sources in S and destinations outside S. Barahona states that an advantage of using these inequalities is that the flow variables are eliminated. On the other hand, testing the cut condition entails solving a max cut problem, which is $\mathcal{NP}$-hard.

Gabrel, Knippel, and Minoux [GKM99] study a multicommodity network design problem similar to, but more general than, Barahona's, in which links of varying capacities are available for construction at varying costs. They discuss an exact solution procedure that uses what they call "bipartition inequalities," which are the cut inequalities of Barahona.

In all of these examples, the inequalities involve the capacity of links leaving the subset, whereas our subset inequalities involve the flow on links leaving the subset.

5.2.3 Results

The structure of our implementation of the subset cuts approach to finding lower bounds is the same as with knapsack cuts: our subset separation routine is added as a CPLEX cut callback and a branch-and-cut process is started, but only the root node is solved.

Back in Section 3.3 we saw the lower bound gaps for the LP relaxation of formulation A on budget FLND and fixed charge FLND in Figures 3.3 and 3.4, respectively. Here we present these curves again, alongside the lower bounds obtained when subset separation is performed, and when CPLEX cuts are added. Figure 5.3 shows lower bounds for budget FLND on our standard test suite. These gaps are 100% when the LP relaxation alone is solved, but are greatly improved when subset cuts are added. Figure 5.4 shows lower bounds for fixed charge FLND; again subset cuts improve the lower bound dramatically. In both problem types, the subset cuts are significantly better than the

5.3. COMPARISON AND DISCUSSION

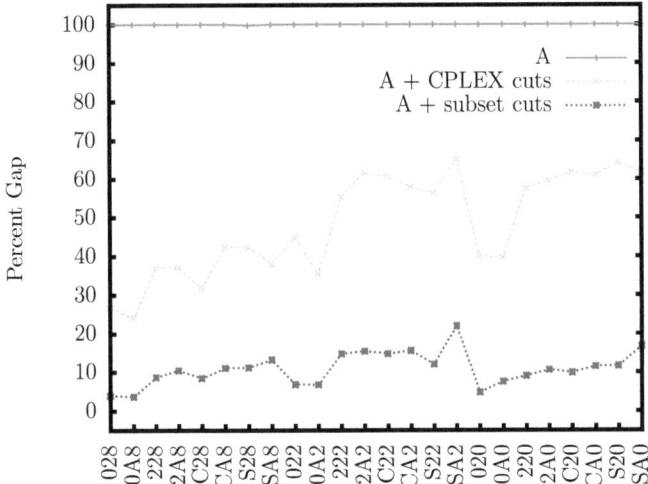

Figure 5.3: Budget FLND: Comparison of lower bounds obtained from solving the root node using the aggregate IP plus various cuts.

CPLEX cuts as well. Tables 5.6 and 5.7 at the end of the chapter give these results in tabular form.

Tables 5.3 and 5.4 summarize the data from the figures for budget and fixed charge FLND, respectively. On average across all the problem instances, solving budget FLND with subset cuts produced lower bound gaps of 10.9%, representing a gap closure of 89% over the LP relaxation alone. If subset cuts and CPLEX cuts are combined, the results are a little better than subset cuts alone, with average lower bound gaps of 9.2%. For fixed charge FLND, the gap closure achieved by the subset cuts was 99.5%, with the remaining gaps less than 1% even in the worst case.

5.3 Comparison and Discussion

Adding knapsack cuts improved the lower bounds calculated using the disaggregate formulation D, and adding subset cuts improved the lower bounds calculated using the aggregate formulation A, but how do they compare to each other? Figure 5.5 illustrates the comparison on budget FLND problems. Formulation D got the better lower bounds, and in fact, the lower bounds of formulation A plus subset cuts were not even as good as the lower bounds from the LP relaxation of D without any cuts added. D is the stronger formulation when it comes to finding lower bounds.

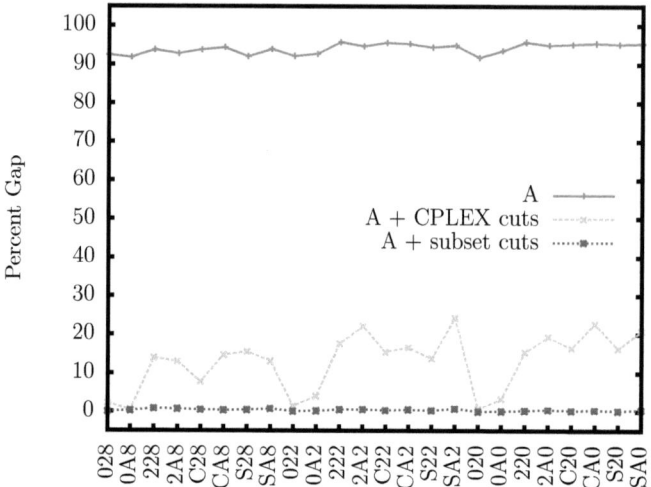

Figure 5.4: Fixed charge FLND: Comparison of lower bounds obtained from solving the root node using the aggregate IP plus various cuts.

Table 5.3: Budget FLND: Summary of root node lower bound gap results using formulation A plus cuts. The last column shows the average gap closure achieved by adding cuts to the LP relaxation.

	Low	Average	High	Gap Closure
A	99.8%	100%	100%	
A + CPLEX cuts	24.1%	48.5%	65.2%	51.5%
A + subset cuts	3.7%	10.9%	22.0%	89.1%
A + CPLEX + subset cuts	0.1%	9.2%	20.5%	90.8%

5.3. COMPARISON AND DISCUSSION

Table 5.4: Fixed charge FLND: Summary of root node lower bound gap results using formulation A plus cuts. The last column shows the average gap closure achieved by adding cuts to the LP relaxation.

	Low	Average	High	Gap Closure
A	91.8%	94.1%	95.8%	
A + CPLEX cuts	0.43%	13.0%	24.3%	86.2%
A + subset cuts	0.01%	0.43%	0.78%	99.5%

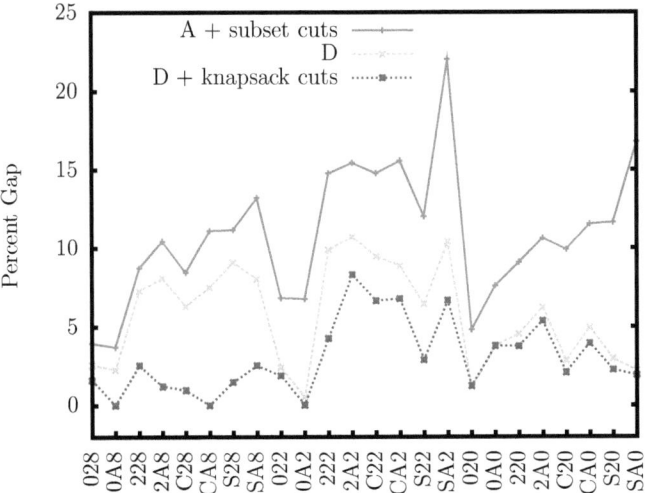

Figure 5.5: Comparison of best lower bound gaps, obtained from LP relaxation of formulation A plus subset cuts and LP relaxation of formulation D plus knapsack cuts, on budget FLND.

Table 5.5: Budget FLND: gaps between optimal solution and lower bound obtained from solving formulation D plus various cuts.

Problem	D	D + CPLEX cuts	D + knapsack ones plus	D + knapsack target
028	2.60%	0.58%	2.55%	1.64%
0A8	2.26%	0.00%	0.12%	0.00%
228	7.28%	3.93%	3.13%	2.56%
2A8	8.10%	3.95%	3.02%	1.21%
C28	6.31%	2.08%	1.46%	0.97%
CA8	7.51%	3.40%	0.65%	0.00%
S28	9.09%	2.67%	2.18%	1.50%
SA8	8.03%	4.00%	3.39%	2.56%
022	2.45%	2.08%	1.92%	1.92%
0A2	0.53%	0.04%	0.05%	0.03%
222	9.89%	6.26%	4.36%	4.28%
2A2	10.75%	9.03%	9.01%	8.31%
C22	9.46%	8.20%	6.91%	6.67%
CA2	8.87%	7.95%	7.82%	6.79%
S22	6.45%	4.95%	3.99%	2.92%
SA2	10.42%	7.84%	7.40%	6.69%
020	1.18%	1.33%	1.30%	1.25%
0A0	3.81%	3.80%	3.81%	3.80%
220	4.55%	4.09%	4.19%	3.77%
2A0	6.24%	6.03%	5.74%	5.38%
C20	2.87%	2.57%	2.63%	2.11%
CA0	4.97%	4.15%	4.10%	3.96%
S20	2.99%	2.52%	2.70%	2.29%
SA0	2.23%	1.80%	2.13%	1.93%

5.3. COMPARISON AND DISCUSSION

Table 5.6: Budget FLND: gaps between optimal solution and lower bound obtained from solving formulation A plus various cuts.

Problem	A	A + CPLEX cuts	A + subset cuts	A + CPLEX and subset cuts
028	100%	26.81%	3.97%	1.78%
0A8	100%	24.07%	3.71%	0.11%
228	100%	37.07%	8.73%	6.25%
2A8	100%	37.16%	10.45%	10.77%
C28	100%	31.86%	8.45%	6.36%
CA8	100%	42.42%	11.12%	8.91%
S28	99.75%	42.31%	11.19%	6.57%
SA8	100%	38.06%	13.22%	7.12%
022	100%	44.83%	6.83%	6.14%
0A2	100%	35.56%	6.78%	2.34%
222	100%	55.40%	14.77%	9.97%
2A2	100%	61.63%	15.44%	13.42%
C22	100%	60.54%	14.77%	12.23%
CA2	100%	58.00%	15.57%	14.80%
S22	100%	56.38%	12.03%	12.14%
SA2	100%	65.16%	22.03%	20.49%
020	100%	39.97%	4.82%	4.70%
0A0	100%	39.68%	7.60%	7.68%
220	100%	57.63%	9.09%	9.10%
2A0	100%	59.61%	10.64%	10.91%
C20	100%	61.73%	9.91%	10.23%
CA0	100%	61.04%	11.55%	11.85%
S20	100%	64.29%	11.65%	11.67%
SA0	100%	61.70%	16.76%	15.89%

Table 5.7: Fixed charge FLND: gaps between optimal solution and lower bound obtained from solving formulation A plus various cuts.

Problem	A	A + CPLEX cuts	A + subset cuts
028	92.49%	2.22%	0.03%
0A8	91.84%	0.43%	0.27%
228	93.79%	13.96%	0.78%
2A8	92.74%	13.01%	0.67%
C28	93.78%	7.78%	0.44%
CA8	94.42%	14.71%	0.35%
S28	92.05%	15.61%	0.43%
SA8	93.92%	13.14%	0.73%
022	92.14%	1.46%	0.08%
0A2	92.68%	4.08%	0.17%
222	95.76%	17.65%	0.50%
2A2	94.70%	22.17%	0.55%
C22	95.61%	15.48%	0.30%
CA2	95.29%	16.67%	0.49%
S22	94.46%	13.80%	0.29%
SA2	94.91%	24.34%	0.76%
020	91.76%	0.72%	0.01%
0A0	93.56%	3.35%	0.09%
220	95.78%	15.46%	0.26%
2A0	94.96%	19.37%	0.48%
C20	95.16%	16.48%	0.21%
CA0	95.44%	22.78%	0.40%
S20	95.17%	16.31%	0.18%
SA0	95.35%	20.91%	0.48%

Chapter 6
Exact Approaches

Putting together the upper and lower bound approaches discussed in Chapters 4 and 5, respectively, this chapter presents an exact branch-and-cut solver for budget FLND. The commercial solver CPLEX works using a branch-and-cut process to solve IPs, and we compare the results of our branch-and-cut approach with those of CPLEX using the default CPLEX settings and cuts.

6.1 A Branch-and-Cut Solver

Our branch-and-cut solver is built on top of CPLEX, taking advantage of the infrastructure already in place in CPLEX. Function calls and cut callbacks are used to customize the branch-and-cut process for FLND problems using our upper and lower bound solution methods.

We formulate the problem using Melkote and Daskin's disaggregate IP formulation. Solving begins by finding a feasible solution using basic variable neighborhood search with step neighborhoods, our best heuristic solver. The objective value of this solution is given as the initial global upper bound for the branch-and-cut process, allowing any tree node with a larger local lower bound to be fathomed immediately. The heuristic is used on the entire problem at the beginning of the process only (not on subproblems).

For use at each node in the branch-and-cut tree, we register with CPLEX a cut callback for knapsack cuts as described in Chapter 5. This callback produces at most one violated knapsack cut based on the current fractional solution each time it is called. The knapsack cuts generated were limited to a maximum of 16 variables. These cuts raise the local lower bound, possibly allowing the node to be fathomed. No other cuts were used.

The variable selection strategy for branching was left up to CPLEX. Initially we tried using various built-in branching strategies by setting parameters in CPLEX, but picking a specific strategy was never better than the "automatic" setting in the cases we tested. With the automatic setting, CPLEX uses an internal algorithm to select the branching strategy based on the problem and its progress. For our problems, CPLEX most often selected variables based on pseudo-shadow prices.

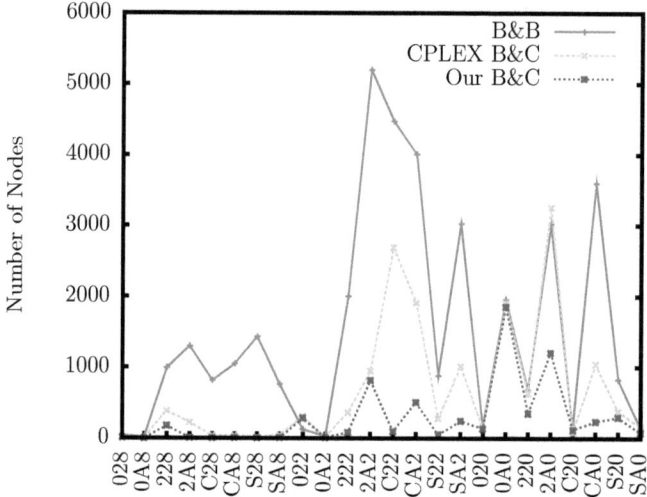

Figure 6.1: Number of nodes in the branch-and-cut tree for exact approaches.

6.2 Results

We solved each problem in the test suite to optimality using each of the following three exact approaches: (1) "Our B&C," the branch-and-cut solver just described, incorporating our upper and lower bound techniques, (2) "CPLEX B&C," the CPLEX IP solver with all the default settings, including CPLEX cuts, and (3) "B&B," the CPLEX IP solver with default settings, but with no cuts, effectively a branch-and-bound approach.

Figure 6.1 shows the number of nodes in the problem tree for each of these approaches. We see clearly that our branch-and-cut approach requires fewer nodes than the branch-and-bound and CPLEX branch-and-cut approaches. On average across all the problem instances, our branch-and-cut requires only 41% of the number of nodes required by the CPLEX branch-and-cut. Table 6.2 at the end of the chapter gives these results in tabular form.

However, the time required for separating the knapsack cuts is significant. Figure 6.2 shows the solve times of the three exact approaches on a logarithmic scale. Our branch-and-cut requires significantly more time, averaging 85 minutes compared to the CPLEX branch-and-cut's average of just under 4 minutes. Table 6.1 summarizes the results from the two figures, giving average number of nodes and solve time in seconds for the three exact approaches across all problem instances.

Partial tests with 19-variable knapsack cuts showed that using more variables in the knapsack separation routine leads to better cuts and fewer nodes in the branch-and-cut

6.2. RESULTS

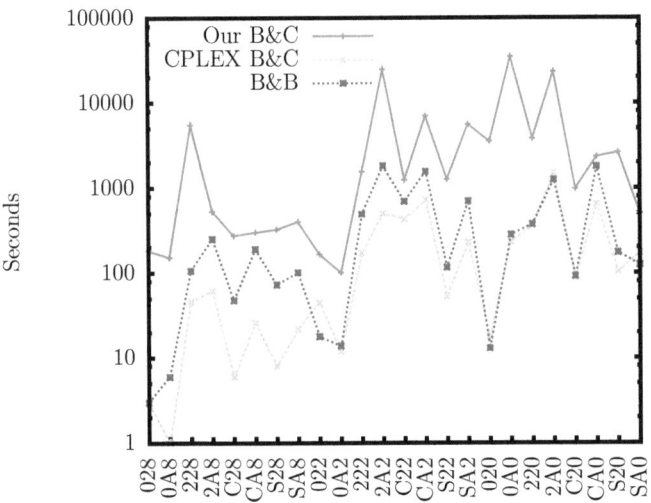

Figure 6.2: Solve times for exact approaches.

tree. However, this also increases the run times significantly.

The power of our branch-and-cut approach to reduce the number of nodes required comes primarily from the knapsack cuts. Using a global upper bound from a heuristic solution helps only a small amount: when the problems were solved with our branch-and-cut using knapsack cuts but no initial global upper bound, the average number of nodes required was 292, compared with 275 when the upper bounds were used. Future work of interest may be developing a heuristic based on a fractional solution that could be used at some of the subproblem nodes to find a feasible solution.

Table 6.1: Average number of nodes in the problem tree and seconds required for solving exact approaches across all problem instances.

	Nodes	Seconds
B&B	1528	431
CPLEX B&C	663	229
Our B&C	275	5089

Table 6.2: Number of nodes in the branch-and-cut tree for exact approaches.

Problem	B&B	CPLEX B&C	Our B&C
028	40	24	10
0A8	17	0	0
228	992	385	177
2A8	1299	224	9
C28	815	36	4
CA8	1049	36	8
S28	1433	18	6
SA8	758	47	9
022	127	304	284
0A2	28	11	10
222	1999	364	82
2A2	5201	947	815
C22	4472	2689	94
CA2	4008	1912	508
S22	878	280	53
SA2	3025	1016	245
020	160	145	137
0A0	1956	1905	1858
220	680	636	352
2A0	3020	3262	1208
C20	140	88	120
CA0	3599	1040	235
S20	824	382	294
SA0	141	163	79

Chapter 7
A Case Study: Nouna

Up to this point we have studied facility location–network design from a mostly theoretical perspective. Now we examine a case study: the application of facility location–network design to a specific real-world setting in order to improve access to facilities. The setting is the Nouna health district of Burkina Faso and the goal is to improve access to health facilities for the people in the district.

Special Acknowledgment

The application of FLND to the Nouna health district was conducted as part of the collaboration between the University of Heidelberg medical school and the CRSN (Nouna Health Research Center) in Nouna. This work could not have been accomplished without the support of these two institutions.

7.1 The Setting: Nouna Health District

The CIA World Factbook describes Burkina Faso, shown in Figure 7.1, as "one of the poorest countries in the world" [CIA08]. The life expectancy is 55 years, the literacy rate is 22%, the unemployment rate is 77%, and 46% of the population lives below the poverty line. The country is landlocked, with limited natural resources, and mostly flat terrain. There are essentially two seasons: the dry season from October to April, with warm temperatures, and the rainy season from May to September, with hot temperatures. Ninety percent of the labor force is involved in agriculture, with cotton being the largest crop [CIA08].

The country is divided into health districts for administering health care, and the Nouna health district, which has the same boundaries as the Kossi political province, lies in the western part of the country, bordering Mali. The terrain is a dry orchard savanna: mostly plains with scattered clumps of trees, and some hills in the northwest. Most of the people are subsistence farmers, and various ethnic groups coexist in the region. Tribal dialects vary and the unifying language is Dioula, a West African trade language. The more educated people also speak French, the official language of Burkina Faso [YSGK02].

Figure 7.1: Burkina Faso. The Nouna health district borders Mali in the western part of the country, just on the other side of the river from Dédougou.

The Nouna health district has 281 population centers, with the town of Nouna, population 21,000, as the capital. The total population in the district is about 275,000, while village populations other than Nouna range from less than 100 to about 6000. There are 25 health facilities scattered throughout the district, including a full hospital at Nouna, and a large health center at Djibasso. Other than these two, the remaining 23 facilities are small, providing basic care. Nouna itself has electrical power 19 hours of the day, but none of the other villages have electricity. A few of the health facilities have solar powered refrigerators for storing medications. Figure 7.2 shows the villages and the road network of Nouna health district, with those villages having a health facility indicated by a lighter color.

Each village is assigned to a particular health facility, although this mapping is not enforced. In some cases, villagers use a facility that is not the one assigned to them. A few villages are located as far away as 45 kilometers by road from their assigned facility. None of the roads in the district are paved, and the dirt roads vary in quality. At the high end are relatively smooth dirt roads with a solid foundation, which do a good job of withstanding rains. At the low end are stretches that are only a "road"

7.1. THE SETTING: NOUNA HEALTH DISTRICT

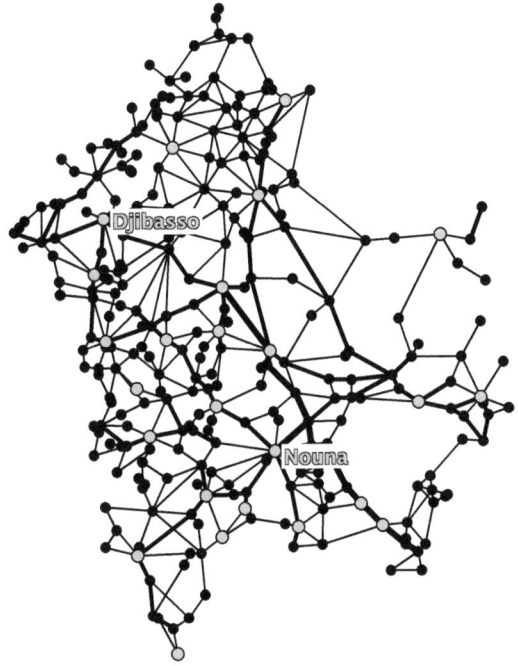

Figure 7.2: Nouna health district, with its 25 health facilities shown.

in that trees have been cleared away. These roads are uneven and poorly marked, and when it rains heavily, as during the rainy season, the dirt turns to a thick mud and they become impassable.

The primary means of transportation in the district are foot, bicycle, and donkey. The donkey is typically not ridden directly, but pulls a cart on which one or more people may ride. Motorbikes are not uncommon, but personal cars are virtually nonexistent.

Health care utilization in Nouna health district is low. Many people prefer the convenience of a village healer, visiting a health facility only in the most serious cases of illness. The time and effort involved in simply traveling to a health facility is a deterrent to seeking proper medical care for many, especially those farthest from a health facility, and especially during the rainy season when travel is most difficult.

7.2 Modeling as FLND

In order to improve the physical access of the people of Nouna health district to the health facilities within district, we can treat the situation as a facility location–network design problem. Our options for improvement include building new facilities and new roads, where building new roads includes upgrading existing roads.

In an application situation, the elements involved may not be easily quantifiable, and in some cases qualitative factors may play an important role. In order to model the situation mathematically, we have to make some simplifying assumptions, and ignore less-pertinent or more-difficult-to-model factors. Thus any results supplied should be interpreted in the wider context and seen as an aid to decision-making rather than a final answer, though they may be provably optimal in the mathematical sense. That being said, such objective results can be a very valuable aid to decision makers, especially in developing countries, where there is much room for improvement and limited resources. Previous studies that have looked specifically at improving access to health facilities in developing countries through strategic location of (additional) health facilities include [CFR06, RS00, O96].

In our study, we do not attempt to model qualitative factors, such as tribal rivalries that sometimes influence which villages a person is willing to visit. We do not account for the differing methods of transportation. Rather, we make the implicit assumption that regardless of the method of transportation, better roads make travel easier.

As is common when working in developing nations, obtaining reliable data on Nouna was not easy. The most recent detailed road map of the area was from 1971, and the records kept by the officials in the district regarding village locations and populations are often hand-written. Additionally, there is seasonal migration of some parts of the population that is not accounted for in the data.

With the caveats given, we have the set of villages in the district, along with their populations, and we know the locations of the 25 existing health facilities. We also have a road map of the district, with three different qualities of road. From this we created the graph shown in Figure 7.2. There are 281 nodes representing the villages, and 475 edges representing the roads. The thicker edges in the graph are higher quality roads. The 25 lighter colored nodes are the locations of existing health facilities.

To translate this into an FLND problem instance, every village is a client node with demand equal to its population. There are 25 existing facilities and 475 existing edges. The travel cost on each edge will be a multiple of its Euclidean length, with three different multiples possible, representing the three different qualities of road. Higher quality roads have smaller multiples, leading to lower travel costs. The travel costs do not have real units, but are a relative measure of the time and effort involved in traveling a road segment.

We may build a new facility at any node that does not already have one. We may build any of a number of different edges, including "upgrades" to existing edges. In real terms, any road that is not already of the highest quality may be upgraded one quality level. In addition to the potential edges representing upgrades to existing roads, we generate the following completely new potential edges: For every pair of nodes without

7.2. MODELING AS FLND

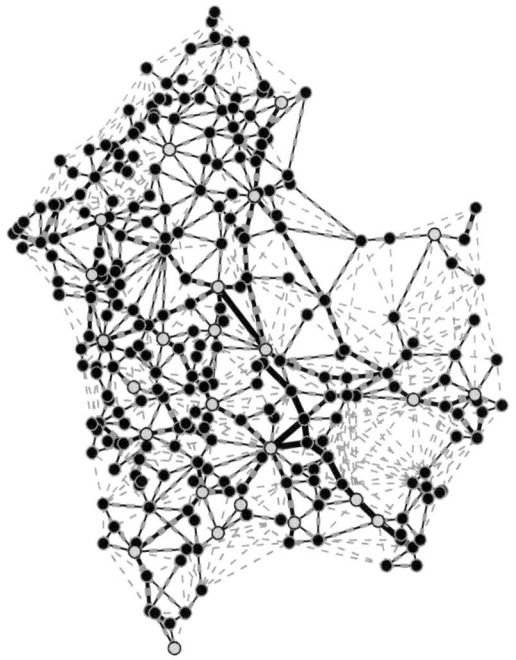

Figure 7.3: The Nouna FLND problem instance. There are 281 nodes, 25 existing facilities, 256 potential facilities, 475 existing edges, and 882 potential edges.

an edge, generate a potential edge if the distance is not more than 1.2 times the longest existing edge, no existing edge is crossed by the potential edge, and no third node lies on, or very near, the potential edge. Using these criteria, there are a total of 882 potential edges. In reality, building a road provides an even greater benefit than we attribute to it in our restricted problem context: roads are traveled for many more reasons than to reach a health facility. Figure 7.3 shows the Nouna FLND problem instance.

In the district, construction costs for health facilities are estimated based on the size of the facility regardless of location. Thus we use uniform construction costs for the potential facilities based on a fixed size facility that can be built at any location. The construction costs of the potential edges are proportional to the length of the edge, with higher quality roads being more expensive. The values used for the construction costs are not in real monetary units, but rather reflect the relative cost of building one element compared to another. Perhaps the least informed estimate we had to make regarded the cost of facilities relative to roads. This choice can influence the number of facilities that will be built in a solution relative to the number of roads. We selected a facility cost that was less than the cost of building the longest roads, but significantly more than the median road construction cost.

With the inputs as described, we have a facility location–network design problem. The objective is to minimize the total travel cost and we have a budget that may be spent constructing facilities and roads. The budget is measured in the same units as the construction costs, and expresses the limited resources that are available. We can plug in different budget values and see what is possible with more or less money.

7.3 Results

Our first step is to evaluate the current setup: according to our model, how "accessible" are the existing 25 facilities for the approximately 275,000 people in the district? The total travel cost is 3.15 million, or 11.49 on average per person. Sixty percent of the population has to travel to another village to visit a health facility and the maximum travel cost is 50. Optimizing these last two measures is not a goal of the model, but we report them as another indicator of the quality of a solution. Because the units of all of these measurements do not correspond directly to a real-world measure, they do not tell us much in and of themselves, but they serve as indicators as we evaluate different solutions.

Before examining solutions involving the construction of additional facilities and roads, we entertained what might have been had FLND been used from the very beginning. Consider the Nouna health district with its current road network but no health facilities, and suppose we have a budget equivalent to the cost of building 25 facilities. Solving this as a budget FLND problem, we can compare the optimal solution produced to the current configuration. Figure 7.4 shows the results. On the left we see the current 25 facilities. On the right we see the optimal solution according to our FLND model: 23 facilities and 25 road segments were selected for construction. The total travel cost of the existing setup is 3.15 million; in the optimal solution on the right, it is 2.43 million, 23% better.

Now we look at improving the current situation by building new facilities and roads. The Nouna instance of FLND, as shown in Figure 7.3, formulated as an integer program using formulation D, could be solved by CPLEX to optimality in time ranging from 90 minutes to 11 hours, depending on the budget. Thus the results we present here are mathematically optimal results.

Figure 7.5 shows the elements selected for construction when the budget is 200. Five facilities and 25 edges are selected. The total travel cost of this solution is 2.22 million, for an average of 8.1, representing a 30% improvement over the current situation. Fifty-five percent of the population, down from 60, must travel to another village to visit a health center, and 33.3, down from 50, is the maximum travel cost anyone has to expend.

Solving the problem for various different budgets gives a number of different possible

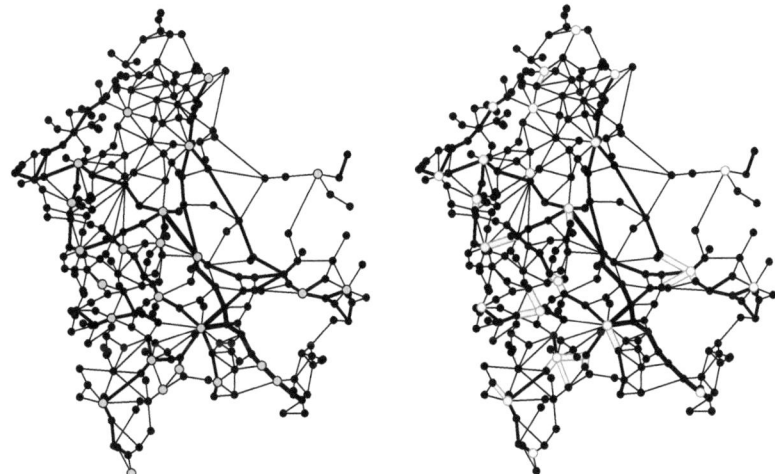

Figure 7.4: The current setup (left) with total travel cost 3.15 million compared with an optimal setup (right) with total travel cost 2.43 million. In the optimal solution, 23 facilities and 25 road segments were selected for construction.

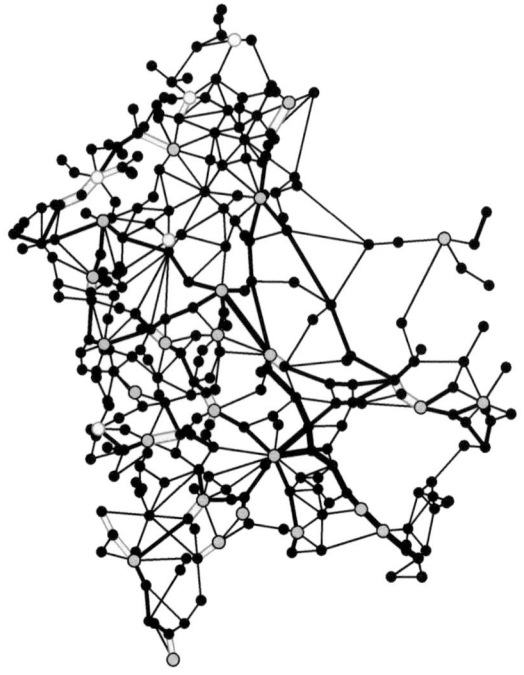

Figure 7.5: The optimal solution with budget 200. Five facilities and 25 edges are selected to be built.

scenarios. Planners need to realize that each solution has a different set of facilities and edges, e. g., the facilities selected in a budget 200 solution do not necessarily include the facilities selected in a budget 100 solution. There may be common elements though, which can provide useful information. For example, the village of Bâ (population 3983) appeared in the solution for every budget we tested, so building a facility there would be effective regardless of the total budget.

The plot in Figure 7.6 (bottom curve) shows how the total travel cost goes down as the budget increases. In the budget 50 solution, one facility and ten edges are built, while in the budget 700 solution, 18 facilities and 83 edges are built. A budget of 540, constructing 13 facilities and 75 edges, cuts the average travel costs for the people in half. This solution, depicted in Figure 7.7, has total travel cost 1.57 million, or average travel cost 5.73, and 52% of the population must travel to another village to visit a health facility. The maximum travel cost is 28.5 units.

7.3. RESULTS

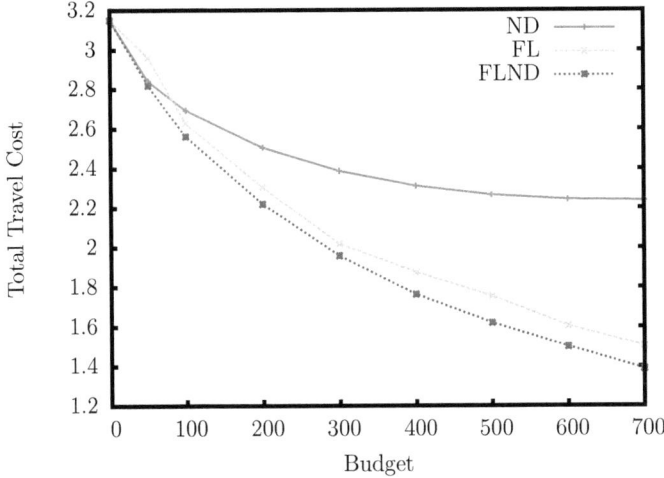

Figure 7.6: Plot of total travel cost as budget increases for the Nouna problem instance, solved as network design, facility location, and facility location–network design.

In order to achieve a total travel cost of 2.43 million, the travel cost of the optimal solution had FLND been used from the beginning, a budget of at least 130 would need to be expended. The budget 130 optimal solution builds 4 additional facilities plus 6 edges and has total travel cost 2.44 million.

Figure 7.6 also includes plots solving the problem as pure facility location and as pure network design. All the same data was used in these cases, but when solving as a facility location problem, we removed all the potential edges so that only facilities could be built. As a network design problem, we removed all the potential facilities so that only edges could be built. The curves show that when considering facility location and network design together, we can make better improvements for the same amount of money as compared with considering either individually.

Table 7.1 shows how many facilities and edges are built in the solutions using various budgets. With a budget of 400, an optimal facility location solution builds 13 facilities, and an optimal network design solution builds 166 roads. The facility location–network design solution makes more efficient use of the budget, building 10 facilities and 49 roads, and achieving a lower total travel cost.

We have seen that applying FLND to health facilities in Nouna health district can make a big difference in the accessibility of the facilities. For the same budget it took to build 25 facilities, one could have built 23 facilities and made some improvements to the road network, and achieved travel costs 23% lower on average. Given the current

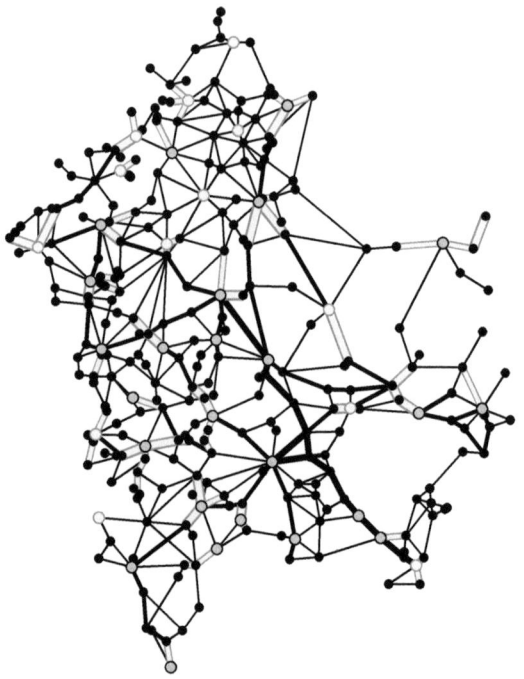

Figure 7.7: The optimal solution with budget 540. Building 13 facilities and 75 edges, this solution cuts the average travel cost in half.

Table 7.1: Comparison of FLND, facility location, and network design with various budgets on the Nouna data. Each entry in the table shows (number of facilities) / (number of edges) in the solution.

Budget	FLND	FL	ND
100	3/6	3/-	-/39
200	5/25	6/-	-/85
300	8/31	10/-	-/122
400	10/49	13/-	-/166
500	12/69	16/-	-/216
600	15/77	20/-	-/246

7.3. RESULTS

situation, a minimum of 4 additional facilities would need to be built, along with a few additional improvements to the road network, in order to achieve a 23% reduction in average travel cost. Building 13 new facilities and 75 new road segments would cut the travel costs in half. Whatever the budget available, our FLND model provides the solution expressing the optimal use of the budget in lowering travel costs, and this information could be a useful aid for the decision makers of Nouna health district.

Chapter 8
Software: FLND Visualizer

As a part of this thesis, we have developed a software application called FLND Visualizer that allows the user to work with FLND problems. The application can read a problem instance from a file or generate one randomly according to user-supplied parameters. Problem instances may be solved using a variety of heuristics, and the solutions can be viewed graphically as well as saved to a file.

The application was written in Java and therefore runs on any platform for which there is a Java virtual machine. It has been tested under Windows XP and SUSE Linux.

Figure 8.1 shows a screenshot of FLND Visualizer. The File menu has choices for starting a new problem instance; opening a problem instance from a file; saving the current instance to a file; exporting the current instance to various formats including pdf, e.g., for printing; and exiting the program. On the right are the controls for working with the problem instance, and the instance itself is displayed as a graph on the large white canvas. A status bar at the bottom displays the name of the problem instance as well as node information for the node that the mouse pointer is currently hovering over, if any.

The top set of controls on the right-hand side allows the user to set the display characteristics of the graph: whether node labels are shown, whether potential edges are shown (if there are many, they can clutter the graph making other elements difficult to see), the diameter of the nodes, and the zoom level.

At the very bottom of the right-hand control panel, information about the graph is displayed, including the number of nodes, edges, and potential edges. The controls displayed in the middle of the panel depend on the user's current task.

8.1 Creating Problem Instances

The user can select the current "view" of the problem instance: "problem" or "solution." The view affects how the problem instance is displayed as well as the available controls for manipulating the problem instance. In problem view, the user can edit the problem instance. In solution view, the user can solve using heuristic methods and view the solutions. When in problem view, as shown in Figure 8.1, the creation controls are

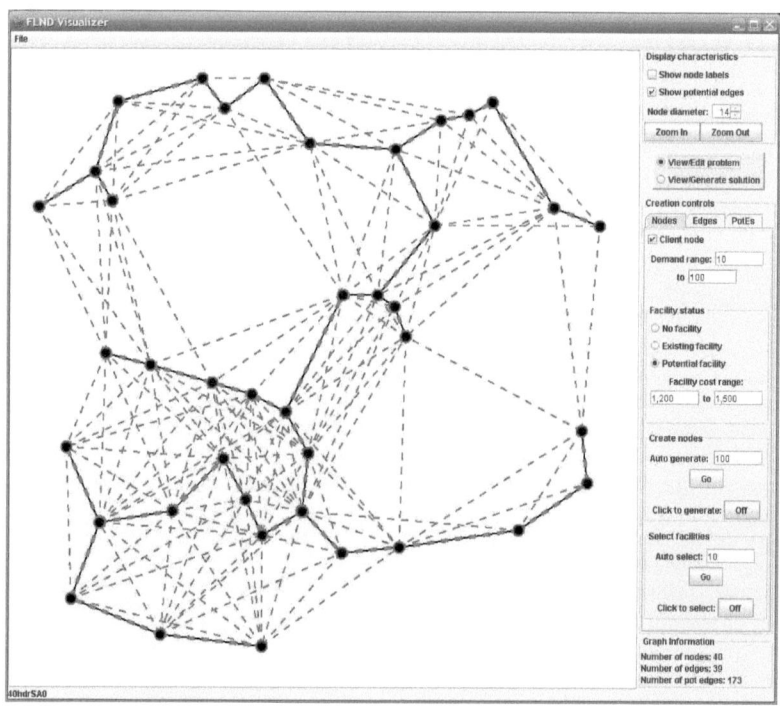

Figure 8.1: FLND Visualizer screenshot: creating a problem instance (under Windows).

shown, with separate tabs for adding nodes, edges, and potentials edges. The nodes tab allows the user to select whether a node is a client or not, and if so, its demand, as well as a node's facility status: no facility, existing facility, or potential facility. The client demands, as well as the construction costs associated with potential facilities, may be set by the user or determined randomly from a specified range. Nodes may be generated manually one at a time by clicking on the canvas, or automatically by randomly placing a user-specified number of nodes at the click of a button.

Likewise edges may be generated one-by-one by selecting two nodes, or automatically. Figure 8.2 shows a screenshot where the user is in the middle of adding edges manually. Automatic generation of edges includes an option for allowing edges to cross each other or not. There is also a "Connect Graph" button that adds the minimal necessary additional edges to connect the graph. The travel cost of an edge is proportional to the length of the edge: the Euclidean length of the edge is multiplied by a "travel cost factor," which the user may specify.

When generating potential edges, the user may generate a specific number, or may click the "Generate All" button to generate all that satisfy certain criteria. The criteria include a user-specified maximum length, not crossing any existing edges, and not passing through a third node. The maximum length is given either as a multiple (e.g., 1.2) of the longest existing edge, or as a percentage of the diagonal of the drawing area. The construction cost of a potential edge is proportional to the length of the edge, being the product of the length of the edge and a "construction cost factor" specified by the user, which may vary by edge.

8.2 Solving and Viewing Solutions

Figure 8.3 shows a screenshot from FLND Visualizer in solution view. On the right-hand control panel the user may select from a variety of heuristic solvers and enter the budget for the problem. Upon clicking the "Solve" button, the problem is solved and the solution displayed on the graph. Elements selected to be in the solution are highlighted. Additionally, solution information is displayed just above the graph information at the bottom on the right: the total travel cost of the solution, total construction cost, and the number of facilities and edges to be built.

The ability to visualize an FLND problem instance can be a great help in understanding and drawing conclusions about the instance. Heuristically solving the instance is a quick way to get a feasible solution and immediately see what it looks like. FLND Visualizer is also an easy way to quickly generate problem instances with desired characteristics. It has been a very handy tool in our own work on FLND problems and could be useful to others working in this area as well.

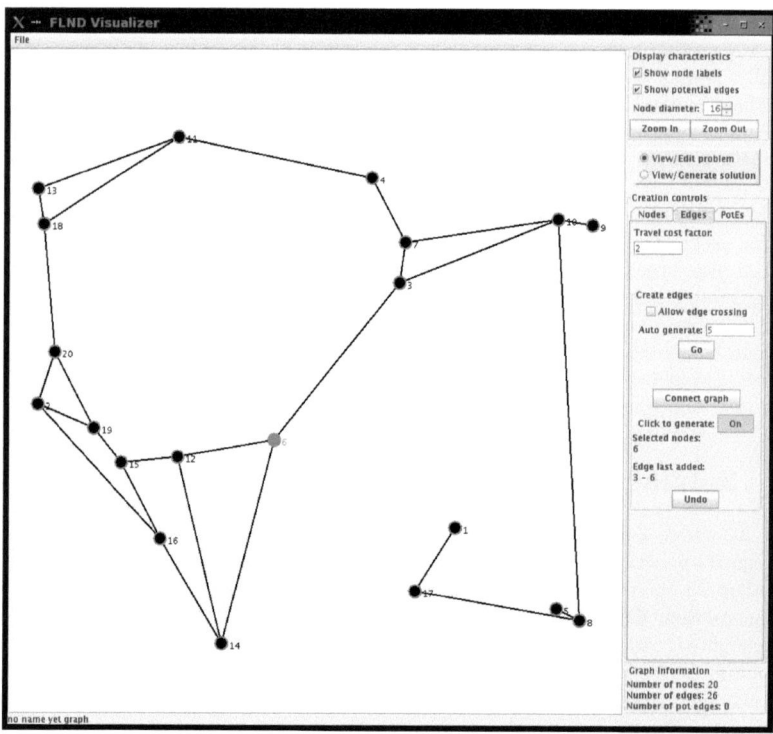

Figure 8.2: FLND Visualizer screenshot: creating a problem instance, adding edges (under Linux).

8.2. SOLVING AND VIEWING SOLUTIONS

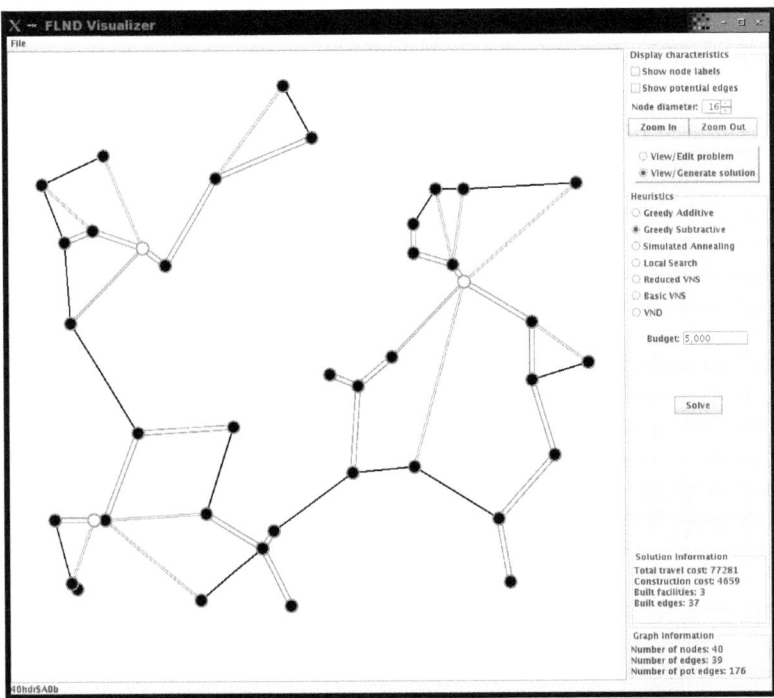

Figure 8.3: FLND Visualizer screenshot: solving a problem instance.

Chapter 9
Discussion and Conclusions

We have presented new solution strategies for solving fixed charge and budget facility location–network design problems. On the upper bound side, we contributed a suite of heuristics for budget FLND, the first in the literature for this problem, for finding good feasible solutions. The basic variable neighborhood search heuristic performed the best, achieving solutions within 0.6% of optimal on average for the problems in our test suite. There were interesting differences among the neighborhood based heuristics: some did better with Hamming neighborhoods and some with step neighborhoods. Future work might explore other types of neighborhoods, or non-neighborhood-based heuristics.

The IP formulation of Melkote and Daskin for fixed charge FLND has an LP relaxation that obtained the optimal solution for the problems in the test suite. However, their IP formulation for budget FLND leaves room for improvement and we contributed a separation routine for knapsack cuts based on the budget. On average, these cuts closed the gap an additional 48%, and in some cases produced the optimal solution. Noting that the knapsack separation routine requires significant time and memory resources, we introduced a more efficient alternative. However, the trade-off produced cuts that were not as good. Investigating efficient methods of generating stronger knapsack cuts may be worthwhile.

Chapter 6 combined our upper and lower bound techniques in an exact branch-and-cut solver using Melkote and Daskin's IP formulation. The number of nodes in the branch-and-cut tree using this solver was much lower than when solving with CPLEX's default branch-and-cut process. One aspect we did not explore that could improve these results further is a clever, problem-specific branching strategy. A heuristic based on a fractional solution for use at subproblem nodes might also deliver improvements.

As an alternative to Melkote and Daskin's IP formulation, we introduced a new IP formulation that aggregates the clients and thus is much smaller, with a linear number of variables and constraints instead of a quadratic number. Using this formulation, some of the problem instances could be solved more quickly (using CPLEX to solve to optimality) than using Melkote and Daskin's formulation. However, the lower bounds produced by the LP relaxation of our aggregate formulation were not nearly as good. We introduced cuts that greatly improve these lower bounds, but not enough to better those obtained from Melkote and Daskin's disaggregate formulation. Future work strengthening the aggregate formulation may result in a more competitive alternative to the disaggregate formulation.

In Chapters 7 and 8 we considered more practical aspects. Chapter 7 examined a case study in which the accessibility of health facilities in Nouna health district was to be improved. We demonstrated the usefulness of FLND results as a decision-making aid in this real-world context. Chapter 8 introduced FLND Visualizer, a software tool for visualizing facility location–network design problem instances and solutions, as well as solving using heuristic methods. This practical tool proved handy countless times in our own work, and could be a help for others studying these problems as well. All the pictures of problem instances in the thesis came from FLND Visualizer.

Individually, facility location and network design have received attention in the combinatorial optimization research community over the years. The combined problem of facility location–network design has received much less attention. FLND is an interesting problem with practical applications. Furthermore, the fact that FLND has facility location and network design as subproblems means it could provide insights into the problems in these separate fields as well. Our work presented in this thesis, coupled with the earlier work of Melkote and Daskin [MD01a, MD01b, MD01c, MD98], provides a solid base and a springboard into deeper pursuits in FLND, a field ripe for further research.

Appendix A
Test Instances

The FLND problem instances described in this appendix are used throughout the thesis when testing our solution methods. As there are no published benchmark instances for facility location–network design, we generated this test suite ourselves. The goal was to create instances with varying characteristics and of a nontrivial size that could be solved by our methods in a reasonable amount of time. Likewise it was important that the instances be solvable to optimality so that results from our solution methods could be effectively evaluated.

The test suite consists of 72 randomly generated instances, using 24 different sets of characteristics. We created three instances, a, b, and c, using each set of characteristics. The computational results presented in the thesis for a given problem instance are an average of the three instances sharing those characteristics.

The following characteristics apply to all problem instances:

- 40 nodes with randomly generated coordinates in a 100 x 100 space
- Every node is a client
- Client demands ranging from 10 to 100
- Potential facility construction costs ranging from 1200 to 1500
- Edge travel costs proportional to length of edge
- Potential edge construction costs proportional to length of edge
- Potential edges satisfy the following criteria: not longer than a certain length, not crossing existing edges, and not passing through a third node

The following characteristics vary:

- Number of existing edges
  - **0**: 0
  - **S**: 39, minimum spanning tree

- **2**: 80, noncrossing ('2' = twice the number of nodes)
- **C**: 80, crossing allowed
- Number of potential edges
  - **2**: 80 ('2' = twice the number of nodes)
  - **A**: All potential edges satisfying the criteria
- Number of existing facilities / potential facilities
  - **0**: 0 / 40
  - **2**: 2 / 38
  - **8**: 8 / 32

The varying characteristics were combined in all possibilities to create the 24 sets of characteristics, and the problem instances are named using the numbers and letters indicated for each characteristic. Thus, S20a, S20b, and S20c refer to instances with existing edges that form a spanning tree, 80 random potential edges, no existing facilities, and 40 potential facilities (one at every node).

When used as budget FLND instances, the following budgets were given for each problem instance:

- Instances 0[2A]0: 8000
- Instances [S2C][2A]0: 6500
- Instances [0S2C][2A][28]: 5000

Tables A.1 and A.2 list all the problem instances, giving for each instance the budget, the number of clients (which is the same as the number of nodes), and the numbers of existing facilities, potential facilities, existing edges, and potential edges. In the case of the instances with no existing edges and 80 randomly generated potential edges, an additional edge sometimes had to be added to ensure that the graph could be connected by the potential edges; otherwise the problem would be infeasible.

The pictures of problem instances displayed in the thesis consistently have the following visual key:

- ● Potential facility
- ○ Existing facility
- ⎯⎯ Existing edge
- ------ Potential edge

Figures A.1 through A.14 show a sampling of the problem instances in graphical form (construction costs, travel costs, and demands not shown).

All the results presented in this thesis come from tests run on machines of the following configuration: 2.8 GHz Intel Xeon processor, 2 GB RAM, running SUSE Linux.

Table A.1: Problem instances, showing for each, the budget, number of clients, number of existing facilities, number of potential facilities, number of existing edges, and number of potential edges.

Instance	Budget	Clients	Ex Facs	Pot Facs	Ex Eds	Pot Eds
020a	8000	40	0	40	0	81
020b	8000	40	0	40	0	80
020c	8000	40	0	40	0	81
022a	5000	40	2	38	0	80
022b	5000	40	2	38	0	80
022c	5000	40	2	38	0	80
028a	5000	40	8	32	0	80
028b	5000	40	8	32	0	80
028c	5000	40	8	32	0	81
0A0a	8000	40	0	40	0	222
0A0b	8000	40	0	40	0	233
0A0c	8000	40	0	40	0	180
0A2a	5000	40	2	38	0	207
0A2b	5000	40	2	38	0	192
0A2c	5000	40	2	38	0	172
0A8a	5000	40	8	32	0	225
0A8b	5000	40	8	32	0	213
0A8c	5000	40	8	32	0	197
220a	6500	40	0	40	80	80
220b	6500	40	0	40	80	80
220c	6500	40	0	40	80	80
222a	5000	40	2	38	80	80
222b	5000	40	2	38	80	80
222c	5000	40	2	38	80	80
228a	5000	40	8	32	80	80
228b	5000	40	8	32	80	80
228c	5000	40	8	32	80	80
2A0a	6500	40	0	40	80	117
2A0b	6500	40	0	40	80	119
2A0c	6500	40	0	40	80	111
2A2a	5000	40	2	38	80	112
2A2b	5000	40	2	38	80	120
2A2c	5000	40	2	38	80	116
2A8a	5000	40	8	32	80	113
2A8b	5000	40	8	32	80	115
2A8c	5000	40	8	32	80	116

Table A.2: Problem instances, showing for each, the budget, number of clients, number of existing facilities, number of potential facilities, number of existing edges, and number of potential edges.

Instance	Budget	Clients	Ex Facs	Pot Facs	Ex Eds	Pot Eds
C20a	6500	40	0	40	80	80
C20b	6500	40	0	40	80	80
C20c	6500	40	0	40	80	80
C22a	5000	40	2	38	80	80
C22b	5000	40	2	38	80	80
C22c	5000	40	2	38	80	80
C28a	5000	40	8	32	80	80
C28b	5000	40	8	32	80	80
C28c	5000	40	8	32	80	80
CA0a	6500	40	0	40	80	120
CA0b	6500	40	0	40	80	130
CA0c	6500	40	0	40	80	125
CA2a	5000	40	2	38	80	117
CA2b	5000	40	2	38	80	145
CA2c	5000	40	2	38	80	132
CA8a	5000	40	8	32	80	124
CA8b	5000	40	8	32	80	128
CA8c	5000	40	8	32	80	139
S20a	6500	40	0	40	39	80
S20b	6500	40	0	40	39	80
S20c	6500	40	0	40	39	80
S22a	5000	40	2	38	39	80
S22b	5000	40	2	38	39	80
S22c	5000	40	2	38	39	80
S28a	5000	40	8	32	39	80
S28b	5000	40	8	32	39	80
S28c	5000	40	8	32	39	80
SA0a	6500	40	0	40	39	173
SA0b	6500	40	0	40	39	176
SA0c	6500	40	0	40	39	147
SA2a	5000	40	2	38	39	161
SA2b	5000	40	2	38	39	182
SA2c	5000	40	2	38	39	157
SA8a	5000	40	8	32	39	177
SA8b	5000	40	8	32	39	171
SA8c	5000	40	8	32	39	160

111

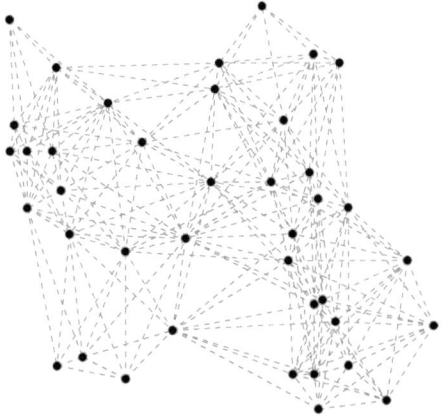

Figure A.1: Problem instance 0A0a.

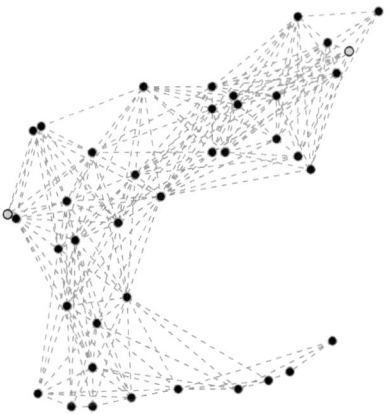

Figure A.2: Problem instance 0A2a.

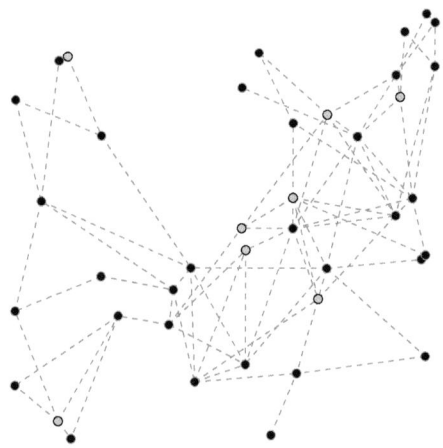

Figure A.3: Problem instance 028a.

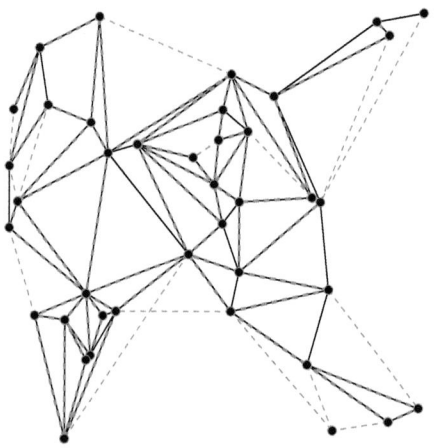

Figure A.4: Problem instance 220c.

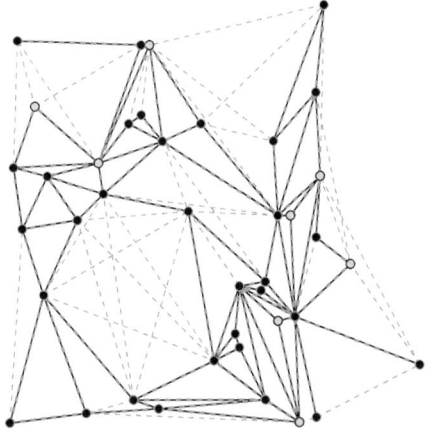

Figure A.5: Problem instance 2A8c.

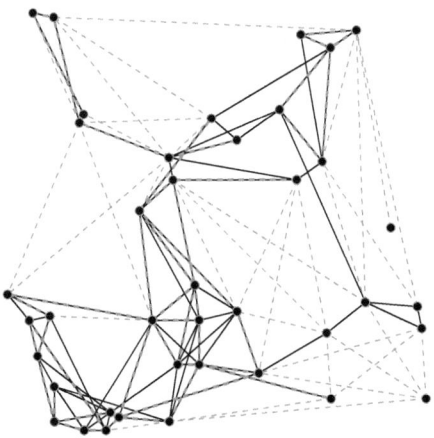

Figure A.6: Problem instance C20a.

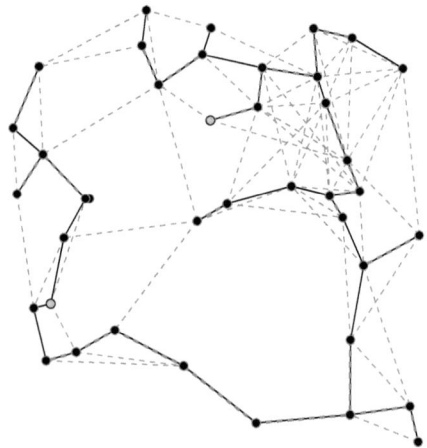

Figure A.7: Problem instance S22b.

Figure A.8: Problem instance S22c.

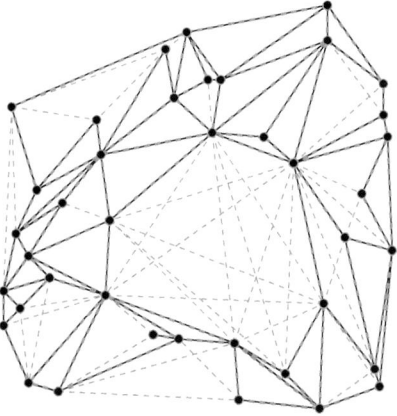

Figure A.9: Problem instance 2A0b.

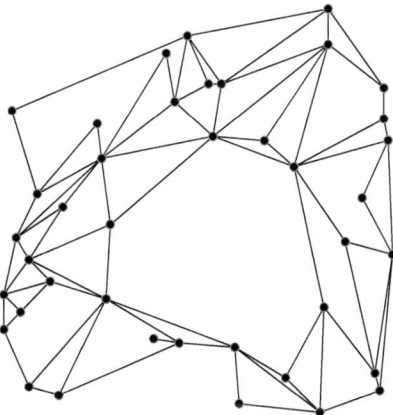

Figure A.10: Problem instance 2A0b without potential edges shown.

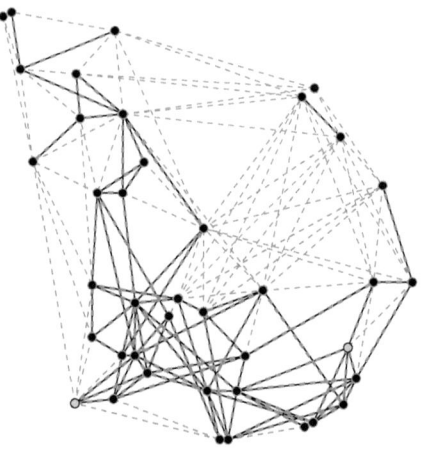

Figure A.11: Problem instance CA2b.

Figure A.12: Problem instance CA2b without potential edges shown.

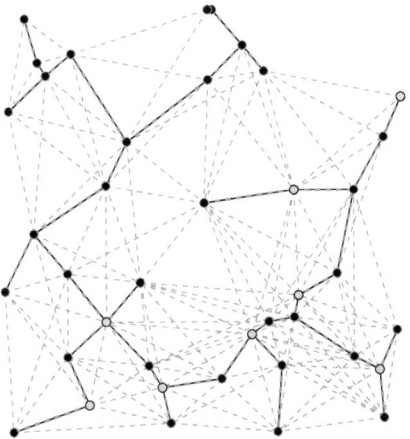

Figure A.13: Problem instance SA8c.

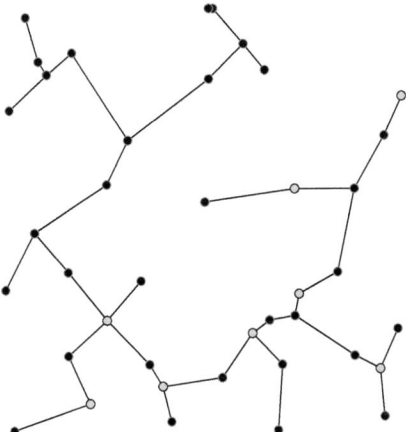

Figure A.14: Problem instance SA8c without potential edges shown.

References

[ABCC01] David Applegate, Robert E. Bixby, Vašek Chvátal, and William Cook. TSP cuts which do not conform to the template paradigm. In M. Jünger and D. Naddef, editors, *Computational Combinatorial Optimization, Optimal or Provably Near-Optimal Solutions*, 261–304, Springer, 2001.

[BMW89] Anantaram Balakrishnan, Thomas L. Magnanti, and Richard T. Wong. A dual-ascent procedure for large-scale uncapacitated network design. *Operations Research* 37(5):716–740, 1989.

[B96] Francisco Barahona. Network design using cut inequalities. *SIAM Journal on Optimization* 6(3):823–837, 1996.

[BIO92] Oded Berman, Divinagracia I. Ingco, and Amedeo R. Odoni. Improving the location of minisum facilities through network modification. *Annals of Operations Research* 40:1–16, 1992.

[BIO94] Oded Berman, Divinagracia I. Ingco, and Amedeo R. Odoni. Improving the location of minimax facilities through network modification. *Networks* 24:31–41, 1994.

[BCG03] Joy Bhadury, Ramaswamy Chandrasekharan, and Laxmi Gewali. Network design subject to facility location. *Proceedings of the 15th Canadian Conference on Computational Geometry*, 128–131, 2003.

[BCG00] Joy Bhadury, Ramaswamy Chandrasekharan, and Laxmi Gewali. Computational complexity of integrated models of network design and facility location. *Southwest Journal of Pure and Applied Mathematics* July 2000(1):30–43, 2000.

[BLO08] Christoph Buchheim, Frauke Liers, and Marcus Oswald. Local cuts revisited. *Operations Research Letters* in press.

[BGH06] Rainer E. Burkard, Elisabeth Gassner, and Johannes Hatzl. A linear time algorithm for the reverse 1-median problem on a cycle. *Networks* 48:16–23, 2006.

[BPZ08] Rainer E. Burkard, Carmen Pleschiutschnig, and Jianzhong Zhang. The inverse 1-median problem on a cycle. *Discrete Optimization* 5(2):242–253, 2008.

[BPZ04]   Rainer E. Burkard, Carmen Pleschiutschnig, and Jianzhong Zhang. Inverse median problems. *Discrete Optimization* 1(1):23–39, 2004.

[CC07]   Xujin Chen and Bo Chen. Approximation algorithms for soft-capacitated facility location in capacitated network design. *Algorithmica* Online First, 2007.

[CIA08]   United States Central Intelligence Agency. The 2008 World Factbook. Web site: www.cia.gov/library/publications/the-world-factbook/.

[C83]   Vašek Chvátal. *Linear Programming.* W.H. Freeman, 1983.

[CFR06]   Cara Cocking, Steffen Flessa, and Gerhard Reinelt. Locating health facilities in Nouna district, Burkina Faso. In H.-D. Haasis, H. Kopfer, and J. Schönberger, editors, *Operations Research Proceedings 2005*, 431–436, Springer, 2006.

[C71]   Stephen A. Cook. The complexity of theorem-proving procedures. *Proceedings of the 3rd Annual ACM Symposium on Theory of Computing*, 151–158, ACM, 1971.

[CLRS01] Thomas H. Cormen, Charles E. Leiserson, Ronald L. Rivest, and Clifford Stein. *Introduction to Algorithms.* MIT Press, 2001.

[CPLEX]   ILOG CPLEX. Web site: www.ilog.com/products/cplex/.

[C88]   John R. Current. The design of a hierarchical transportation network with transshipment facilities. *Transportation Science* 22(4):270–277, 1988.

[CDS02]   John R. Current, Mark S. Daskin, and David A. Schilling. Discrete network location models. In Drezner and Hamacher, editors, *Facility Location*, 81–118, Springer, 2002.

[CP91]   John R. Current and Hasan Pirkul. The hierarchical network design problem with transshipment facilities. *European Journal of Operational Research* 51(3):338–347, 1991.

[D51]   George B. Dantzig. Maximization of a linear function of variables subject to linear inequalities. In T.C. Koopmans, editor, *Activity Analysis of Production and Allocation*, 359–373. Wiley, 1951.

[D95]   Mark S. Daskin. *Network and Discrete Location: Models, Algorithms, and Applications.* Wiley-Interscience, 1995.

[D06]   Reinhard Diestel. *Graph Theory.* Springer, 2006.

[DW03]   Zvi Drezner and George O. Wesolowsky. Network design: Selection and design of links and facility location. *Transportation Research Part A* 37:241–256, 2003.

REFERENCES

[GKM99]   Virginie Gabrel, Arnaud Knippel, and Michel Minoux. Exact solution of multicommodity network optimization problems with general step cost functions. *Operations Research Letters* 25:15–23, 1999.

[GJ79]   Michael R. Garey and David S. Johnson. *Computers and Intractability: A Guide to the Theory of NP-Completeness.* W.H. Freeman, 1979.

[H64]   S.L. Hakimi. Optimum locations of switching centers and the absolute centers and medians of a graph. *Operations Research* 12:450–459, 1964.

[H65]   S.L. Hakimi. Optimum distribution of switching centers in a communication network and some related graph theoretic problems. *Operations Research* 13:462–475, 1965.

[HBUM07]   Pierre Hansen, Jack Brimberg, Dragan Urošević, and Nenad Mladenović. Primal-dual variable neighborhood search for the simple plant-location problem. *INFORMS Journal on Computing* 19(4):552–564, 2007.

[HM01]   Pierre Hansen and Nenad Mladenović. Variable neighborhood search: Principles and applications. *European Journal of Operational Research* 130:449–467, 2001.

[HM03]   Pierre Hansen and Nenad Mladenović. Variable neighborhood search. In F. Glover and G. Kochenberger, editors, *Handbook of Metaheuristics*, 145–184, Springer, 2003.

[HM97]   Pierre Hansen and Nenad Mladenović. Variable neighborhood search for the p-median. *Location Science* 5(4):207–226, 1997.

[HMP01]   Pierre Hansen, Nenad Mladenović, and Dionisio Perez-Brito. Variable neighborhood decomposition search. *Journal of Heuristics* 7(4):335–350, 2001.

[H04]   Clemens Heuberger. Inverse combinatorial optimization: a survey on problems, methods, and results. *Journal of Combinatorial Optimization* 8:329–361, 2004.

[H03]   Juraj Hromkovič. *Algorithmics for Hard Problems: Introduction to Combinatorial Optimization, Randomization, Approximation, and Heuristics.* Springer, 2003.

[JRT95]   Michael Jünger, Gerhard Reinelt, and Stefan Thienel. Problem solving with cutting plane algorithms in combinatorial optimization. In W. Cook, L. Lovász, and P. Seymour, editors, *Combinatorial Optimization, Papers from the DIMACS Special Year*, volume 20 of *DIMACS Series in Discrete Mathematics and Theoretical Computer Science*, 111–152, American Mathematical Society, 1995.

REFERENCES

[K98]   John G. Klincewicz. Hub location in backbone/tributary network design: A review. *Location Science* 6:307–335, 1998.

[MW84]   Thomas L. Magnanti and Richard T. Wong. Network design and transportation planning: models and algorithms. *Transportation Science* 18(1):1–55, 1984.

[M64]   F.E. Maranzana. On the location of supply points to minimize transport costs. *OR*, 15(3):261–270, 1964.

[MS02]   Vladimir Marianov and Daniel Serra. Location problems in the public sector. In Drezner and Hamacher, editors, *Facility Location*, 119–150, Springer, 2002.

[MG08]   Inmaculada Rodríguez Martín and Juan José Salazar González. Solving a capacitated hub location problem. *European Journal of Operational Research* 184(2):468–479, 2008.

[M04]   James McCaffrey Generating the mth lexicographical element of a mathematical combination. *Visual Studio Technical Articles*, 2004, available at http://msdn.microsoft.com/en-us/library/aa289166(VS.71).aspx.

[MD01a]   Sanjay Melkote and Mark S. Daskin. An integrated model of facility location and transportation network design. *Transportation Research*, 35(6):515–538, 2001.

[MD01b]   Sanjay Melkote and Mark S. Daskin. Capacitated facility location/network design problems. *European Journal of Operational Research*, 129:481–495, 2001.

[MD01c]   Sanjay Melkote and Mark S. Daskin. Polynomially solvable cases of combined facility location-network design problems. Technical Report, 2001.

[MD98]   Sanjay Melkote and Mark S. Daskin. The maximum covering facility location-network design problem. Technical Report, 1998.

[MH97a]   Nenad Mladenović and Pierre Hansen. Variable neighborhood search. *Computers and Operations Research* 24(11):1097–1100, 1997.

[O96]   Joseph R. Oppong. Accommodating the rainy season in third world location-allocation applications. *Socio-Economic Planning Sciences* 30(2):121–137, 1996.

[RS00]   Shams-Ur Rahman and David K. Smith. Use of location-allocation models in health service development planning in developing nations. *European Journal of Operational Research* 123:437–452, 2000.

REFERENCES

[RS06]   R. Ravi and Amitabh Sinha. Approximation algorithms for problems combining facility location and network design. *Operations Research* 54(1):73–81, 2006.

[RW03]   Mauricio G.C. Resende and Renato F. Werneck. On the implementation of a swap-based local search procedure for the p-median problem. In R.E. Ladner, editor, *Proceedings of the Fifth Workshop on Algorithm Engineering and Experiments (ALENEX '03) SIAM*, 119–127, 2003.

[RE05]   Charles S. ReVelle and Horst A. Eiselt. Location analysis: A synthesis and survey *European Journal of Operational Research* 165:1–19, 2005.

[RED08] Charles S. ReVelle, Horst A. Eiselt, and Mark S. Daskin. A bibliography for some fundamental problem categories in discrete location science *European Journal of Operational Research* 184:817–848, 2008.

[SJB93] David A. Schilling, Vaidyanathan Jayaraman, and Reza Barkhi. A review of covering problems in facility location. *Location Science* 1(1):25–55, 1993.

[TB68]   Michael B. Teitz and Polly Bart. Heuristic methods for estimating the generalized vertex median of a weighted graph. *Operations Research* 16:955–961, 1968.

[W83]   R.A. Whitaker. A fast algorithm for the greedy interchange for large-scale clustering and median location problems. *INFOR* 21(2):95–108, 1983.

[W98]   Laurence A. Wolsey. *Integer Programming*. Wiley-Interscience, 1998.

[YSGK02] Yazoumé Yé, Aboubakary Sanou, Adjima Gbangou, and Bocar Kouyaté. Nouna DSS, Burkina Faso. In O.A. Sankoh et al., editors, *Population and Health in Developing Countries*, 221–226, International Development Research Centre, 2002.

[ZLM00] Jianzhong Zhang, Zhenhong Liu, and Zhongfan Ma. Some reverse location problems. *European Journal of Operational Research* 124(1):77–88, 2000.

Südwestdeutscher Verlag
für Hochschulschriften

Wissenschaftlicher Buchverlag bietet
kostenfreie
Publikation
von
Dissertationen und Habilitationen

Sie verfügen über eine wissenschaftliche Abschlußarbeit zu aktuellen oder zeitlosen Fragestellungen, die hohen inhaltlichen und formalen Anspruchen genügt, und haben **Interesse an einer honorarvergüteten Publikation?**

Dann senden Sie bitte erste Informationen über Ihre Arbeit per Email an: info@svh-verlag.de.

Unser Außenlektorat meldet sich umgehend bei Ihnen.

Südwestdeutscher Verlag für Hochschulschriften
Aktiengesellschaft & Co. KG
Dudweiler Landstr. 99
D – 66123 Saarbrücken
www.svh-verlag.de

Printed by Books on Demand GmbH, Norderstedt / Germany